INTERNATIONAL PROFESSIONAL PRACTICES FRAMEWORK (IPPF)®

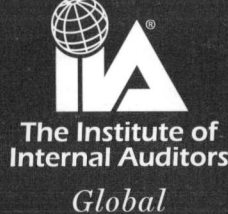

The Institute of Internal Auditors

Global

Copyright © 2017 by The Institute of Internal Auditors, Inc., its successors or assigns ("The IIA"). All rights reserved.

Permission has been obtained from the copyright holder, The IIA, 1035 Greenwood Blvd., Suite 401, Lake Mary, Florida 32746, U.S.A. to publish this reproduction, which is the same in all material respects, as the original unless approved as changed.

The IIA publishes this document for informational and educational purposes. This document is intended to provide information, but is not a substitute for legal or accounting advice. The IIA does not provide such advice and makes no warranty as to any legal or accounting results through its publication of this document. When legal or accounting issues arise, professional assistance should be sought and retained.

The Institute of Internal Auditors
1035 Greenwood Blvd., Suite 401
Lake Mary, FL 32746, USA

For professional guidance, comments, and suggestions, send an email to guidance@theiia.org. To find out about future updates to the IPPF, interested parties are encouraged to monitor the Professional Guidance pages at global.theiia.org.

ISBN: 978-0-89413-984-0

2017 Edition First Printing

Table of Contents

Acknowledgements 13
About The IIA 13
About the IPPF 15
Mission of Internal Audit 21
Core Principles for the Professional Practice of Internal Auditing 25
Definition of Internal Auditing 29
The Code of Ethics 33
    Introduction to the Code of Ethics 33
    Applicability and Enforcement of the Code of Ethics 33
    Principles 34
    Rules of Conduct 35

International Standards for the Professional Practice of Internal Auditing (Standards) 38
    Introduction to the *Standards* 38

Attribute Standards 41
    1000 – Purpose, Authority, and Responsibility 41
    1010 – Recognizing Mandatory Guidance in the Internal Audit Charter 41
    1100 – Independence and Objectivity 42
    1110 – Organizational Independence 42
    1111 – Direct Interaction with the Board 43
    1112 – Chief Audit Executive Roles Beyond Internal Auditing 43

1120 – Individual Objectivity 43
1130 – Impairment to Independence or Objectivity 44
1200 – Proficiency and Due Professional Care 45
1210 – Proficiency 45
1220 – Due Professional Care 46
1230 – Continuing Professional Development 46
1300 – Quality Assurance and Improvement Program 47
1310 – Requirements of the Quality Assurance and Improvement Program 47
1311 – Internal Assessments 47
1312 – External Assessments 48
1320 – Reporting on the Quality Assurance and Improvement Program 48
1321 – Use of "Conforms with the *International Standards for the Professional Practice of Internal Auditing*" 49
1322 – Disclosure of Nonconformance 49

Performance Standards 50

2000 – Managing the Internal Audit Activity 50
2010 – Planning 50
2020 – Communication and Approval 51
2030 – Resource Management 51
2040 – Policies and Procedures 51
2050 – Coordination and Reliance 51
2060 – Reporting to Senior Management and the Board 52
2070 – External Service Provider and Organizational Responsibility for Internal Auditing 53
2100 – Nature of Work 53
2110 – Governance 53

2120 – Risk Management 54
2130 – Control 55
2200 – Engagement Planning 55
2201 – Planning Considerations 56
2210 – Engagement Objectives 56
2220 – Engagement Scope 57
2230 – Engagement Resource Allocation 57
2240 – Engagement Work Program 58
2300 – Performing the Engagement 58
2310 – Identifying Information 58
2320 – Analysis and Evaluation 58
2330 – Documenting Information 59
2340 – Engagement Supervision 59
2400 – Communicating Results 59
2410 – Criteria for Communicating 59
2420 – Quality of Communications 60
2421 – Errors and Omissions 61
2430 – Use of "Conducted in Conformance with the *International Standards for the Professional Practice of Internal Auditing*" 61
2431 – Engagement Disclosure of Nonconformance 61
2440 – Disseminating Results 61
2450 – Overall Opinions 62
2500 – Monitoring Progress 62
2600 – Communicating the Acceptance of Risks 63

Implementation Guidance 66
IG1000 – Purpose, Authority, and Responsibility 66
IG1010 – Recognizing Mandatory Guidance in the Internal Audit Charter 69

IG1100 – Independence and Objectivity	71
IG1110 – Organizational Independence	75
IG1111 – Direct Interaction with the Board	78
IG1112 – Chief Audit Executive Roles Beyond Internal Auditing	80
IG1120 – Individual Objectivity	84
IG1130 – Impairment to Independence or Objectivity	87
IG1200 – Proficiency and Due Professional Care	90
IG1210 – Proficiency	93
IG1220 – Due Professional Care	97
IG1230 – Continuing Professional Development	100
IG1300 – Quality Assurance and Improvement Program	103
IG1310 – Requirements of the Quality Assurance and Improvement Program	108
IG1311 – Internal Assessments	111
IG1312 – External Assessments	116
IG1320 – Reporting on the Quality Assurance and Improvement Program	121
IG1321 – Use of "Conforms with the *International Standards for the Professional Practice of Internal Auditing*"	126
IG1322 – Disclosure of Nonconformance	129
IG2000 – Managing the Internal Audit Activity	132
IG2010 – Planning	136
IG2020 – Communication and Approval	139
IG2030 – Resource Management	142
IG2040 – Policies and Procedures	144
IG2050 – Coordination and Reliance	147
IG2060 – Reporting to Senior Management and the Board	151
IG2070 – External Service Provider and Organizational Responsibility for Internal Auditing	157

IG2100 – Nature of Work	161
IG2110 – Governance	164
IG2120 – Risk Management	170
IG2130 – Control	174
IG2200 – Engagement Planning	178
IG2201 – Planning Considerations	181
IG2210 – Engagement Objectives	184
IG2220 – Engagement Scope	186
IG2230 – Engagement Resource Allocation	188
IG2240 – Engagement Work Program	191
IG2300 – Performing the Engagement	193
IG2310 – Identifying Information	197
IG2320 – Analysis and Evaluation	200
IG2330 – Documenting Information	205
IG2340 – Engagement Supervision	208
IG2400 – Communicating Results	211
IG2410 – Criteria for Communicating	213
IG2420 – Quality of Communications	216
IG2421 – Errors and Omissions	219
IG2430 – Use of "Conducted in Conformance with the International Standards for the Professional Practice of Internal Auditing"	221
IG2431 – Engagement Disclosure of Nonconformance	223
IG2440 – Disseminating Results	226
IG2450 – Overall Opinions	229
IG2500 – Monitoring Progress	232
IG2600 – Communicating the Acceptance of Risk	235

Glossary 238

Table of Contents (Flash Drive)

Supplemental Guidance

Practice Guides

    Assessing Organizational Governance in the Private Sector

    Assessing the Adequacy of Risk Management Using ISO 31000

    Assisting Small Internal Audit Activities in Implementing the International Standards for the Professional Practice of Internal Auditing

    Audit Reports: Communicating Assurance Results

    Auditing Anti-bribery and Anti-corruption Programs

    Auditing Executive Compensation and Benefits

    Auditing External Business Relationships

    Auditing Privacy Risks, 2nd Edition

    Auditing the Control Environment

    Business Continuity Management

    Chief Audit Executives—Appointment, Performance, Evaluation, and Termination

    Coordinating Risk Management and Assurance

    Developing the Internal Audit Strategic Plan

    Evaluating Corporate Social Responsibility/Sustainable Development

    Evaluating Ethics-related Programs and Activities

    Formulating and Expressing Internal Audit Opinions

    Independence and Objectivity

    Integrated Auditing

    Interaction with the Board

Internal Audit and the Second Line of Defense

Internal Auditing and Fraud

Measuring Internal Audit Effectiveness and Efficiency

Quality Assurance and Improvement Program

Reliance by Internal Audit on Other Assurance Providers

Selecting, Using, and Creating Maturity Models: A Tool for Assurance and Consulting Engagements

Talent Management

Practice Guides—Public Sector

Assessing Organizational Governance in the Public Sector

Creating an Internal Audit Competency Process for the Public Sector

Global Technology Audit Guide (GTAG)

Assessing Cybersecurity Risk: Roles of the Three Lines of Defense

Auditing Application Controls

Auditing IT Governance

Auditing IT Projects

Auditing Smart Devices: An Internal Auditor's Guide to Understanding and Auditing Smart Devices

Auditing User-developed Applications

Business Continuity Management

Change and Patch Management Controls: Critical for Organizational Success, 2nd Edition

Continuous Auditing: Coordinating Continuous Auditing and Monitoring to Provide Continuous Assurance, 2nd Edition

Data Analysis Technologies

Developing the IT Audit Plan

Fraud Prevention and Detection in an Automated World

Identity and Access Management
Information Security Governance
Information Technology Outsourcing, 2nd Edition
Information Technology Risk and Controls, 2nd Edition
Management of IT Auditing, 2nd Edition

Guide to the Assessment of IT Risk (GAIT)

GAIT Methodology
GAIT for IT General Control Deficiency Assessment
GAIT for Business and IT Risk

Acknowledgements

The Institute of Internal Auditors (IIA) is grateful to those government agencies, professional organizations, internal and external auditors, and members of management, boards of directors, and academe who provided guidance and assistance in the development and interpretation of the International Professional Practices Framework (IPPF). The IIA is deeply indebted to those individuals who served on the IPPF Oversight Council, Professional Practices Advisory Council, Professional Guidance Advisory Council, the Professional Responsibilities and Ethics Committee, the International Internal Audit Standards Board, and Guidance Development Committee, Information Technology Guidance Committee, Financial Services Guidance Committee and Financial Services Guidance Committee.

About The IIA

The Institute of Internal Auditors (IIA) is the internal audit profession's most widely recognized advocate, educator, and provider of standards, guidance, and certifications. Established in 1941, The IIA today serves more than 185,000 members from more than 170 countries and territories. The Institute's global headquarters are in Lake Mary, Fla., USA. For more information, visit www.globaliia.org.

About the IPPF

In general, a framework provides a structural blueprint of how a body of knowledge and guidance fit together. As a coherent system, a framework facilitates consistent development, interpretation, and application of concepts, methodologies, and techniques useful to a discipline or profession. Specifically, the purpose of the International Professional Practices Framework (IPPF) is to organize The Institute of Internal Auditors' (IIA's) authoritative guidance in a manner that is readily accessible on a timely basis while strengthening the position of The IIA as the standard-setting body for the internal audit profession globally. By encompassing current internal audit practice as well as allowing for future expansion, the IPPF is intended to assist practitioners and stakeholders throughout the world in being responsive to the expanding market for high quality internal auditing.

Throughout the world, internal auditing is performed in diverse environments and within organizations that vary in purpose, size, and structure. In addition, the laws and customs within various countries differ from one another. These differences may affect the practice of internal auditing in each environment. The implementation of the IPPF, therefore, will be governed by the environment in which the internal audit activity carries out its assigned responsibilities. No information contained within the IPPF should be construed in a manner that conflicts with applicable laws or regulations. If a situation arises where information contained within the IPPF may be in conflict with legislation or regulation, internal auditors are encouraged to contact The IIA or legal counsel for further guidance.

The mandatory nature of the *Standards* is emphasized by the use of the word "must." The *Standards* use the word "must" to specify an unconditional requirement. In some exceptional cases, the *Standards* use the term "should." The *Standards* use the word "should" where conformance is expected unless, when applying professional judgment, circumstances justify deviation.

Elements	Definition
Mission of Internal Audit	The Mission of Internal Audit articulates what internal audit aspires to accomplish within an organization. Its place in the IPPF is deliberate, demonstrating how practitioners should leverage the entire framework to facilitate their ability to achieve the Mission.
Core Principles for the Professional Practice of Internal Auditing	The Core Principles, taken as a whole, articulate internal audit effectiveness. For an internal audit function to be considered effective, all Principles should be present and operating effectively. How an internal auditor, as well as an internal audit activity, demonstrates achievement of the Core Principles may be quite different from organization to organization, but failure to achieve any of the Principles would imply that an internal audit activity was not as effective as it could be in achieving internal audit's mission (see Mission of Internal Audit).
Definition of Internal Auditing	Internal auditing is an independent, objective assurance and consulting activity designed to add value and improve an organization's operations. It helps an organization accomplish its objectives by bringing a systematic, disciplined approach to evaluate and improve the effectiveness of risk management, control, and governance processes.
Code of Ethics	The Code of Ethics states the principles and expectations governing behavior of individuals and organizations in the conduct of internal auditing. It describes the minimum requirements for conduct, and behavioral expectations rather than specific activities.
International Standards for the Professional Practice of Internal Auditing (Standards)	The *Standards* are a set of principles-based, mandatory requirements consisting of: • Statements of core requirements for the professional practice of internal auditing and for evaluating the effectiveness of performance that are internationally applicable at organizational and individual levels. • Interpretations clarifying terms or concepts within the Standard

The left side of the table is labeled **Mandatory Guidance** (covering Core Principles, Definition of Internal Auditing, Code of Ethics, and International Standards).

	Elements	Definition
Recommended Guidance	**Implementation Guidance**	Implementation Guides and Practice Advisories assist internal auditors in applying the Standards. They collectively address internal auditing's approach, methodologies, and consideration, but do not detail processes or procedures.
	Supplemental Guidance	Supplemental Guidance provides detailed guidance for conducting internal audit activities. These include topical areas, sector-specific issues, as well as processes and procedures, tools and techniques, programs, step-by-step approaches, and examples of deliverables. Supplemental Guidance includes Practice Guides, Practice Guides: Financial Services, Practice Guides: Public Sector, Global Technology Audit Guides (GTAGs), and Guides to the Assessment of IT Risks (GAIT) as part of Supplemental Guidance.

While endorsed by The IIA and developed by an IIA international guidance committees and/or institute following due process, recommended guidance is not mandatory and has been developed to provide a wide range of applicable solutions to meet the requirements of The IIA's mandatory guidance. The IIA recommends that independent expert advice be sought relating directly to any specific situation.

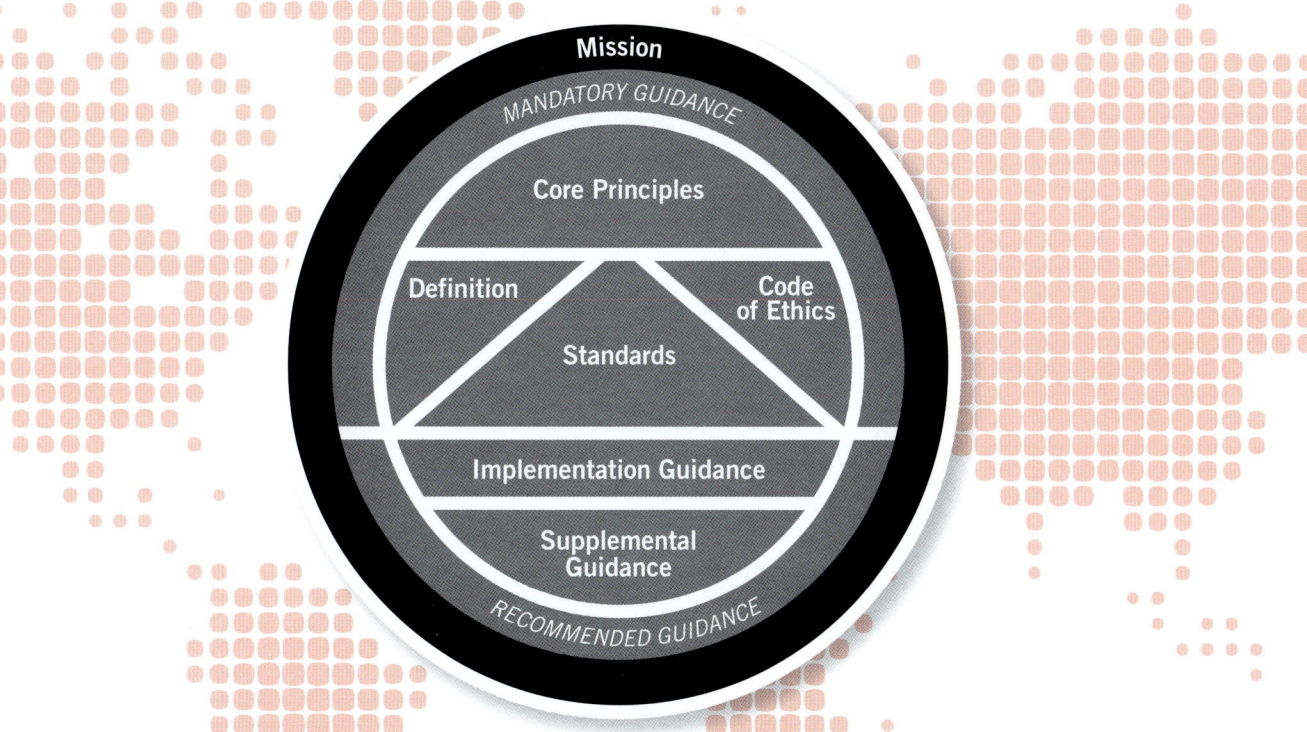

Mission of Internal Audit

Mission of Internal Audit

"To enhance and protect organizational value by providing risk-based and objective assurance, advice, and insight."

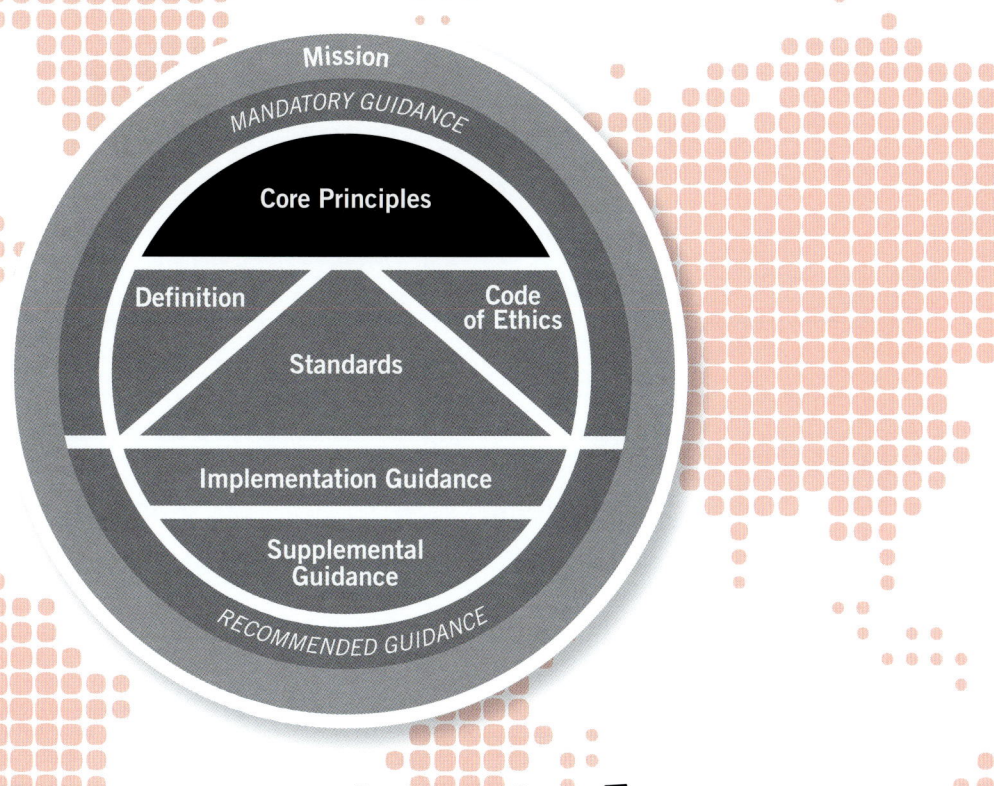

Core Principles

| Mission | **Core Principles** | Definition | Code of Ethics |

Core Principles for the Professional Practice of Internal Auditing

- Demonstrates integrity.
- Demonstrates competence and due professional care.
- Is objective and free from undue influence (independent).
- Aligns with the strategies, objectives, and risks of the organization.
- Is appropriately positioned and adequately resourced.
- Demonstrates quality and continuous improvement.
- Communicates effectively.
- Provides risk-based assurance.
- Is insightful, proactive, and future-focused.
- Promotes organizational improvement.

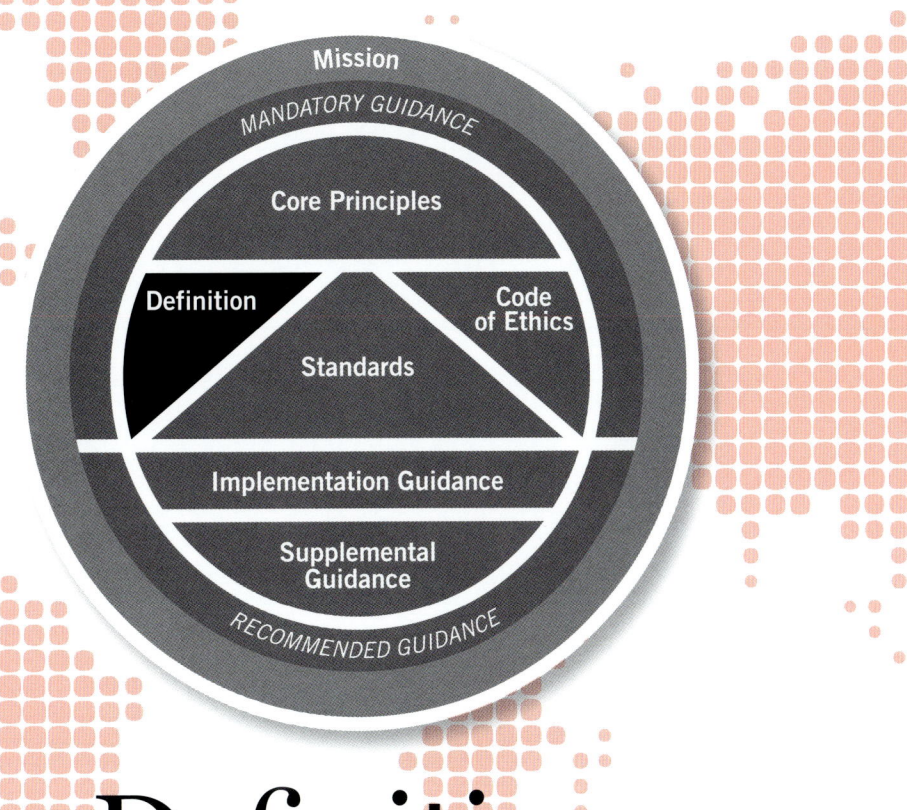

Definition

| Mission | Core Principles | Definition | Code of Ethics |

Definition of Internal Auditing

Internal auditing is an independent, objective assurance and consulting activity designed to add value and improve an organization's operations. It helps an organization accomplish its objectives by bringing a systematic, disciplined approach to evaluate and improve the effectiveness of risk management, control, and governance processes.

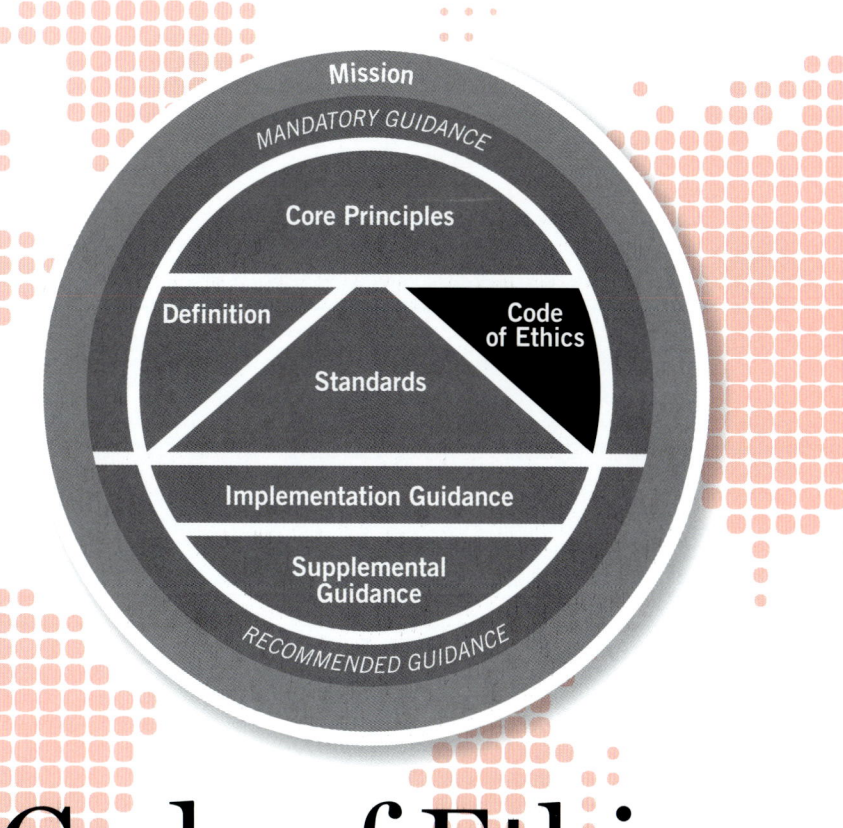

Code of Ethics

Mission | Core Principles | Definition | Code of Ethics

Code of Ethics

Introduction to the Code of Ethics

The purpose of The Institute's Code of Ethics is to promote an ethical culture in the profession of internal auditing.

> *Internal auditing is an independent, objective assurance and consulting activity designed to add value and improve an organization's operations. It helps an organization accomplish its objectives by bringing a systematic, disciplined approach to evaluate and improve the effectiveness of risk management, control, and governance processes.*

A code of ethics is necessary and appropriate for the profession of internal auditing, founded as it is on the trust placed in its objective assurance about governance, risk management, and control.

The Institute's Code of Ethics extends beyond the Definition of Internal Auditing to include two essential components:

1. Principles that are relevant to the profession and practice of internal auditing.
2. Rules of Conduct that describe behavior norms expected of internal auditors. These rules are an aid to interpreting the Principles into practical applications and are intended to guide the ethical conduct of internal auditors.

"Internal auditors" refers to Institute members, recipients of or candidates for IIA professional certifications, and those who perform internal audit services within the Definition of Internal Auditing.

Applicability and Enforcement of the Code of Ethics

This Code of Ethics applies to both entities and individuals that perform internal audit services.

For IIA members and recipients of or candidates for IIA professional certifications, breaches of the Code of Ethics will be evaluated and administered according to The Institute's Bylaws and Administrative Directives. The fact that a particular conduct is not mentioned in the Rules of Conduct does not prevent it from being unacceptable or discreditable, and therefore, the member, certification holder, or candidate can be liable for disciplinary action.

| Mission | Core Principles | Definition | Code of Ethics |

Principles

Internal auditors are expected to apply and uphold the following principles:

1. Integrity

The integrity of internal auditors establishes trust and thus provides the basis for reliance on their judgment.

2. Objectivity

Internal auditors exhibit the highest level of professional objectivity in gathering, evaluating, and communicating information about the activity or process being examined. Internal auditors make a balanced assessment of all the relevant circumstances and are not unduly influenced by their own interests or by others in forming judgments.

3. Confidentiality

Internal auditors respect the value and ownership of information they receive and do not disclose information without appropriate authority unless there is a legal or professional obligation to do so.

4. Competency

Internal auditors apply the knowledge, skills, and experience needed in the performance of internal audit services.

Standards   Implementation Guidance   Glossary

Rules of Conduct

1. Integrity

Internal auditors:

1.1 Shall perform their work with honesty, diligence, and responsibility.
1.2 Shall observe the law and make disclosures expected by the law and the profession.
1.3 Shall not knowingly be a party to any illegal activity or engage in acts that are discreditable to the profession of internal auditing or to the organization.
1.4 Shall respect and contribute to the legitimate and ethical objectives of the organization.

2. Objectivity

Internal auditors:

2.1 Shall not participate in any activity or relationship that may impair, or be presumed to impair their unbiased assessment. This participation includes those activities or relationships that may be in conflict with the interests of the organization.
2.2 Shall not accept anything that may impair, or be presumed to impair their professional judgment.
2.3 Shall disclose all material facts known to them that, if not disclosed, may distort the reporting of activities under review.

3. Confidentiality

Internal auditors:

3.1 Shall be prudent in the use and protection of information acquired in the course of their duties.
3.2 Shall not use information for any personal gain or in any manner that would be contrary to the law or detrimental to the legitimate and ethical objectives of the organization.

4. Competency

Internal auditors:

4.1 Shall engage only in those services for which they have the necessary knowledge, skills, and experience.
4.2 Shall perform internal audit services in accordance with the International Standards for the Professional Practice of Internal Auditing.
4.3 Shall continually improve their proficiency and the effectiveness and quality of their services.

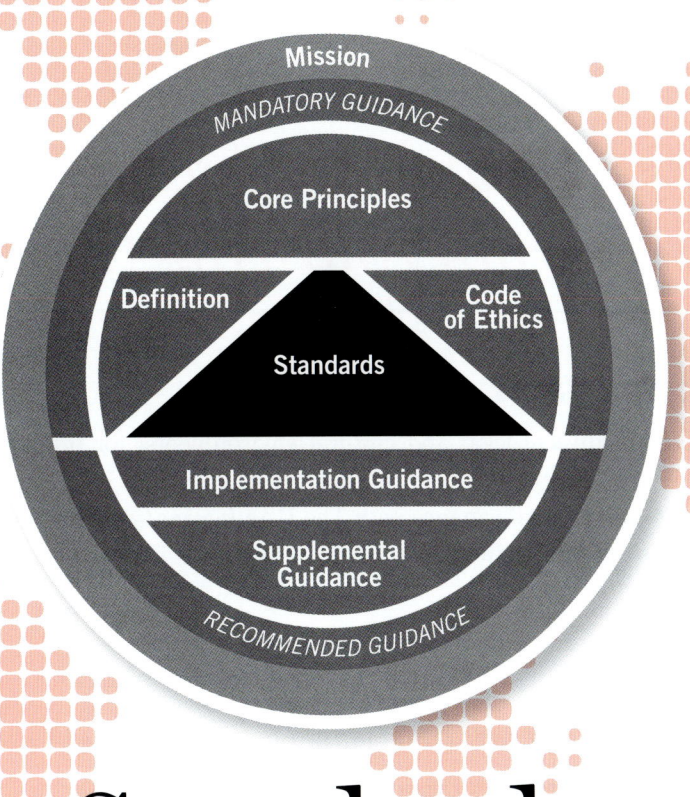

Standards

| Mission | Core Principles | Definition | Code of Ethics |

International Standards for the Professional Practice of Internal Auditing (Standards)

Introduction to the *Standards*

Internal auditing is conducted in diverse legal and cultural environments; for organizations that vary in purpose, size, complexity, and structure; and by persons within or outside the organization. While differences may affect the practice of internal auditing in each environment, conformance with The IIA's *International Standards for the Professional Practice of Internal Auditing* (*Standards*) is essential in meeting the responsibilities of internal auditors and the internal audit activity.

The purpose of the *Standards* is to:

1. Guide adherence with the mandatory elements of the International Professional Practices Framework.

2. Provide a framework for performing and promoting a broad range of value-added internal auditing services.

3. Establish the basis for the evaluation of internal audit performance.

4. Foster improved organizational processes and operations.

| Standards | Implementation Guidance | Glossary |

The *Standards* are a set of principles-based, mandatory requirements consisting of:

- Statements of core requirements for the professional practice of internal auditing and for evaluating the effectiveness of performance that are internationally applicable at organizational and individual levels.
- Interpretations clarifying terms or concepts within the *Standards*.

The *Standards*, together with the Code of Ethics, encompass all mandatory elements of the International Professional Practices Framework; therefore, conformance with the Code of Ethics and the *Standards* demonstrates conformance with all mandatory elements of the International Professional Practices Framework.

The *Standards* employ terms as defined specifically in the Glossary. To understand and apply the *Standards* correctly, it is necessary to consider the specific meanings from the Glossary. Furthermore, the *Standards* use the word "must" to specify an unconditional requirement and the word "should" where conformance is expected unless, when applying professional judgment, circumstances justify deviation.

The *Standards* comprise two main categories: Attribute and Performance Standards. Attribute Standards address the attributes of organizations and individuals performing internal auditing. Performance Standards describe the nature of internal auditing and provide quality criteria against which the performance of these services can be measured. Attribute and Performance Standards apply to all internal audit services.

Implementation Standards expand upon the Attribute and Performance Standards by providing the requirements applicable to assurance (.A) or consulting (.C) services.

Assurance services involve the internal auditor's objective assessment of evidence to provide opinions or conclusions regarding an entity, operation, function, process, system, or other subject matters. The nature and scope of an assurance engagement are determined by the internal auditor. Generally, three parties are participants in assurance services: (1) the person or group directly involved with the entity, operation, function, process, system, or other subject matter—the process owner, (2) the person or group making the assessment—the internal auditor, and (3) the person or group using the assessment—the user.

Consulting services are advisory in nature and are generally performed at the specific request of an engagement client. The nature and scope of the consulting engagement are subject to agreement with the engagement client. Consulting services generally involve two parties: (1) the person or group offering the advice—the internal auditor, and (2) the person or group seeking and receiving the advice—the engagement client. When performing consulting services the internal auditor should maintain objectivity and not assume management responsibility.

| Mission | Core Principles | Definition | Code of Ethics |

The *Standards* apply to individual internal auditors and the internal audit activity. All internal auditors are accountable for conforming with the *Standards* related to individual objectivity, proficiency, due professional care, and the *Standards* relevant to the performance of their job responsibilities. Chief audit executives are additionally accountable for the internal audit activity's overall conformance with the *Standards*.

If internal auditors or the internal audit activity is prohibited by law or regulation from conformance with certain parts of the *Standards*, conformance with all other parts of the *Standards* and appropriate disclosures are needed.

If the *Standards* are used in conjunction with requirements issued by other authoritative bodies, internal audit communications may also cite the use of other requirements, as appropriate. In such a case, if the internal audit activity indicates conformance with the *Standards* and inconsistencies exist between the *Standards* and other requirements, internal auditors and the internal audit activity must conform with the *Standards* and may conform with the other requirements if such requirements are more restrictive.

The review and development of the *Standards* is an ongoing process. The International Internal Audit Standards Board engages in extensive consultation and discussion before issuing the *Standards*. This includes worldwide solicitation for public comment through the exposure draft process. All exposure drafts are posted on The IIA's website as well as being distributed to all IIA institutes.

Suggestions and comments regarding the *Standards* can be sent to:

The Institute of Internal Auditors
Standards and Guidance
1035 Greenwood Boulevard, Suite 401
Lake Mary, FL 32746, USA

E-mail: guidance@theiia.org
Web: www.globaliia.org

Attribute Standards

1000 — Purpose, Authority, and Responsibility

The purpose, authority, and responsibility of the internal audit activity must be formally defined in an internal audit charter, consistent with the Mission of Internal Audit and the mandatory elements of the International Professional Practices Framework (the Core Principles for the Professional Practice of Internal Auditing, the Code of Ethics, the *Standards*, and the Definition of Internal Auditing). The chief audit executive must periodically review the internal audit charter and present it to senior management and the board for approval.

Interpretation:

The internal audit charter is a formal document that defines the internal audit activity's purpose, authority, and responsibility. The internal audit charter establishes the internal audit activity's position within the organization, including the nature of the chief audit executive's functional reporting relationship with the board; authorizes access to records, personnel, and physical properties relevant to the performance of engagements; and defines the scope of internal audit activities. Final approval of the internal audit charter resides with the board.

> **1000.A1** – The nature of assurance services provided to the organization must be defined in the internal audit charter. If assurances are to be provided to parties outside the organization, the nature of these assurances must also be defined in the internal audit charter.

> **1000.C1** – The nature of consulting services must be defined in the internal audit charter.

1010 — Recognizing Mandatory Guidance in the Internal Audit Charter

The mandatory nature of the Core Principles for the Professional Practice of Internal Auditing, the Code of Ethics, the *Standards*, and the Definition of Internal Auditing must be recognized in the internal audit charter. The chief audit executive should discuss the Mission of Internal Audit and the mandatory elements of the International Professional Practices Framework with senior management and the board.

1100 — Independence and Objectivity

The internal audit activity must be independent, and internal auditors must be objective in performing their work.

Interpretation:

Independence is the freedom from conditions that threaten the ability of the internal audit activity to carry out internal audit responsibilities in an unbiased manner. To achieve the degree of independence necessary to effectively carry out the responsibilities of the internal audit activity, the chief audit executive has direct and unrestricted access to senior management and the board. This can be achieved through a dual-reporting relationship. Threats to independence must be managed at the individual auditor, engagement, functional, and organizational levels.

Objectivity is an unbiased mental attitude that allows internal auditors to perform engagements in such a manner that they believe in their work product and that no quality compromises are made. Objectivity requires that internal auditors do not subordinate their judgment on audit matters to others. Threats to objectivity must be managed at the individual auditor, engagement, functional, and organizational levels.

1110 — Organizational Independence

The chief audit executive must report to a level within the organization that allows the internal audit activity to fulfill its responsibilities. The chief audit executive must confirm to the board, at least annually, the organizational independence of the internal audit activity.

Interpretation:

Organizational independence is effectively achieved when the chief audit executive reports functionally to the board. Examples of functional reporting to the board involve the board:

- *Approving the internal audit charter.*
- *Approving the risk-based internal audit plan.*
- *Approving the internal audit budget and resource plan.*
- *Receiving communications from the chief audit executive on the internal audit activity's performance relative to its plan and other matters.*
- *Approving decisions regarding the appointment and removal of the chief audit executive.*

- *Approving the remuneration of the chief audit executive.*
- *Making appropriate inquiries of management and the chief audit executive to determine whether there are inappropriate scope or resource limitations.*

1110.A1 – The internal audit activity must be free from interference in determining the scope of internal auditing, performing work, and communicating results. The chief audit executive must disclose such interference to the board and discuss the implications.

1111—Direct Interaction with the Board

The chief audit executive must communicate and interact directly with the board.

1112—Chief Audit Executive Roles Beyond Internal Auditing

Where the chief audit executive has or is expected to have roles and/or responsibilities that fall outside of internal auditing, safeguards must be in place to limit impairments to independence or objectivity.

Interpretation:

The chief audit executive may be asked to take on additional roles and responsibilities outside of internal auditing, such as responsibility for compliance or risk management activities. These roles and responsibilities may impair, or appear to impair, the organizational independence of the internal audit activity or the individual objectivity of the internal auditor. Safeguards are those oversight activities, often undertaken by the board, to address these potential impairments, and may include such activities as periodically evaluating reporting lines and responsibilities and developing alternative processes to obtain assurance related to the areas of additional responsibility.

1120—Individual Objectivity

Internal auditors must have an impartial, unbiased attitude and avoid any conflict of interest.

Interpretation:

Conflict of interest is a situation in which an internal auditor, who is in a position of trust, has a competing professional or personal interest. Such competing interests can make it difficult to fulfill his or her duties impartially. A conflict of interest exists even if no unethical or improper act results. A conflict of interest can create an appearance of impropriety that can undermine confidence in the internal auditor, the internal audit activity, and the profession. A conflict of interest could impair an individual's ability to perform his or her duties and responsibilities objectively.

1130—Impairment to Independence or Objectivity

If independence or objectivity is impaired in fact or appearance, the details of the impairment must be disclosed to appropriate parties. The nature of the disclosure will depend upon the impairment.

Interpretation:

Impairment to organizational independence and individual objectivity may include, but is not limited to, personal conflict of interest, scope limitations, restrictions on access to records, personnel, and properties, and resource limitations, such as funding.

The determination of appropriate parties to which the details of an impairment to independence or objectivity must be disclosed is dependent upon the expectations of the internal audit activity's and the chief audit executive's responsibilities to senior management and the board as described in the internal audit charter, as well as the nature of the impairment.

1130.A1 – Internal auditors must refrain from assessing specific operations for which they were previously responsible. Objectivity is presumed to be impaired if an internal auditor provides assurance services for an activity for which the internal auditor had responsibility within the previous year.

1130.A2 – Assurance engagements for functions over which the chief audit executive has responsibility must be overseen by a party outside the internal audit activity.

1130.A3 – The internal audit activity may provide assurance services where it had previously performed consulting services, provided the nature of the consulting did not impair objectivity and provided individual objectivity is managed when assigning resources to the engagement.

1130.C1 – Internal auditors may provide consulting services relating to operations for which they had previous responsibilities.

1130.C2 – If internal auditors have potential impairments to independence or objectivity relating to proposed consulting services, disclosure must be made to the engagement client prior to accepting the engagement.

International Professional Practices Framework

1200—Proficiency and Due Professional Care

Engagements must be performed with proficiency and due professional care.

1210—Proficiency

Internal auditors must possess the knowledge, skills, and other competencies needed to perform their individual responsibilities. The internal audit activity collectively must possess or obtain the knowledge, skills, and other competencies needed to perform its responsibilities.

Interpretation:

Proficiency is a collective term that refers to the knowledge, skills, and other competencies required of internal auditors to effectively carry out their professional responsibilities. It encompasses consideration of current activities, trends, and emerging issues, to enable relevant advice and recommendations. Internal auditors are encouraged to demonstrate their proficiency by obtaining appropriate professional certifications and qualifications, such as the Certified Internal Auditor designation and other designations offered by The Institute of Internal Auditors and other appropriate professional organizations.

> **1210.A1** – The chief audit executive must obtain competent advice and assistance if the internal auditors lack the knowledge, skills, or other competencies needed to perform all or part of the engagement.
>
> **1210.A2** – Internal auditors must have sufficient knowledge to evaluate the risk of fraud and the manner in which it is managed by the organization, but are not expected to have the expertise of a person whose primary responsibility is detecting and investigating fraud.
>
> **1210.A3** – Internal auditors must have sufficient knowledge of key information technology risks and controls and available technology-based audit techniques to perform their assigned work. However, not all internal auditors are expected to have the expertise of an internal auditor whose primary responsibility is information technology auditing.
>
> **1210.C1** – The chief audit executive must decline the consulting engagement or obtain competent advice and assistance if the internal auditors lack the knowledge, skills, or other competencies needed to perform all or part of the engagement.

1220—Due Professional Care

Internal auditors must apply the care and skill expected of a reasonably prudent and competent internal auditor. Due professional care does not imply infallibility.

1220.A1 – Internal auditors must exercise due professional care by considering the:

- *Extent of work needed to achieve the engagement's objectives.*
- *Relative complexity, materiality, or significance of matters to which assurance procedures are applied.*
- *Adequacy and effectiveness of governance, risk management, and control processes.*
- *Probability of significant errors, fraud, or noncompliance.*
- *Cost of assurance in relation to potential benefits.*

1220.A2 – In exercising due professional care internal auditors must consider the use of technology-based audit and other data analysis techniques.

1220.A3 – Internal auditors must be alert to the significant risks that might affect objectives, operations, or resources. However, assurance procedures alone, even when performed with due professional care, do not guarantee that all significant risks will be identified.

1220.C1 – Internal auditors must exercise due professional care during a consulting engagement by considering the:

- *Needs and expectations of clients, including the nature, timing, and communication of engagement results.*
- *Relative complexity and extent of work needed to achieve the engagement's objectives.*
- *Cost of the consulting engagement in relation to potential benefits.*

1230—Continuing Professional Development

Internal auditors must enhance their knowledge, skills, and other competencies through continuing professional development.

1300—Quality Assurance and Improvement Program

The chief audit executive must develop and maintain a quality assurance and improvement program that covers all aspects of the internal audit activity.

Interpretation:

A quality assurance and improvement program is designed to enable an evaluation of the internal audit activity's conformance with the Standards *and an evaluation of whether internal auditors apply the Code of Ethics. The program also assesses the efficiency and effectiveness of the internal audit activity and identifies opportunities for improvement. The chief audit executive should encourage board oversight in the quality assurance and improvement program.*

1310—Requirements of the Quality Assurance and Improvement Program

The quality assurance and improvement program must include both internal and external assessments.

1311—Internal Assessments

Internal assessments must include:

- Ongoing monitoring of the performance of the internal audit activity.
- Periodic self-assessments or assessments by other persons within the organization with sufficient knowledge of internal audit practices.

Interpretation:

Ongoing monitoring is an integral part of the day-to-day supervision, review, and measurement of the internal audit activity. Ongoing monitoring is incorporated into the routine policies and practices used to manage the internal audit activity and uses processes, tools, and information considered necessary to evaluate conformance with the Code of Ethics and the Standards.

Periodic assessments are conducted to evaluate conformance with the Code of Ethics, and the Standards.

Sufficient knowledge of internal audit practices requires at least an understanding of all elements of the International Professional Practices Framework.

1312—External Assessments

External assessments must be conducted at least once every five years by a qualified, independent assessor or assessment team from outside the organization. The chief audit executive must discuss with the board:

- The form and frequency of external assessment.
- The qualifications and independence of the external assessor or assessment team, including any potential conflict of interest.

Interpretation:

External assessments may be accomplished through a full external assessment, or a self-assessment with independent external validation. The external assessor must conclude as to conformance with the Code of Ethics and the Standards; *the external assessment may also include operational or strategic comments.*

A qualified assessor or assessment team demonstrates competence in two areas: the professional practice of internal auditing and the external assessment process. Competence can be demonstrated through a mixture of experience and theoretical learning. Experience gained in organizations of similar size, complexity, sector or industry, and technical issues is more valuable than less relevant experience. In the case of an assessment team, not all members of the team need to have all the competencies; it is the team as a whole that is qualified. The chief audit executive uses professional judgment when assessing whether an assessor or assessment team demonstrates sufficient competence to be qualified.

An independent assessor or assessment team means not having either an actual or a perceived conflict of interest and not being a part of, or under the control of, the organization to which the internal audit activity belongs. The chief audit executive should encourage board oversight in the external assessment to reduce perceived or potential conflicts of interest.

1320—Reporting on the Quality Assurance and Improvement Program

The chief audit executive must communicate the results of the quality assurance and improvement program to senior management and the board. Disclosure should include:

- The scope and frequency of both the internal and external assessments.
- The qualifications and independence of the assessor(s) or assessment team, including potential conflicts of interest.

- Conclusions of assessors.
- Corrective action plans.

Interpretation:

The form, content, and frequency of communicating the results of the quality assurance and improvement program is established through discussions with senior management and the board and considers the responsibilities of the internal audit activity and chief audit executive as contained in the internal audit charter. To demonstrate conformance with the Code of Ethics and the Standards, *the results of external and periodic internal assessments are communicated upon completion of such assessments and the results of ongoing monitoring are communicated at least an`nually. The results include the assessor's or assessment team's evaluation with respect to the degree of conformance.*

1321—Use of "Conforms with the *International Standards for the Professional Practice of Internal Auditing*"

Indicating that the internal audit activity conforms with the *International Standards for the Professional Practice of Internal Auditing* is appropriate only if supported by the results of the quality assurance and improvement program.

Interpretation:

The internal audit activity conforms with the Code of Ethics and the Standards *when it achieves the outcomes described therein. The results of the quality assurance and improvement program include the results of both internal and external assessments. All internal audit activities will have the results of internal assessments. Internal audit activities in existence for at least five years will also have the results of external assessments.*

1322—Disclosure of Nonconformance

When nonconformance with the Code of Ethics or the *Standards* impacts the overall scope or operation of the internal audit activity, the chief audit executive must disclose the nonconformance and the impact to senior management and the board.

Performance Standards

2000—Managing the Internal Audit Activity

The chief audit executive must effectively manage the internal audit activity to ensure it adds value to the organization.

Interpretation:

The internal audit activity is effectively managed when:

- *It achieves the purpose and responsibility included in the internal audit charter.*
- *It conforms with the* Standards.
- *Its individual members conform with the Code of Ethics and the* Standards.
- *It considers trends and emerging issues that could impact the organization.*

The internal audit activity adds value to the organization and its stakeholders when it considers strategies, objectives, and risks; strives to offer ways to enhance governance, risk management and control processes; and objectively provides relevant assurance.

2010—Planning

The chief audit executive must establish a risk-based plan to determine the priorities of the internal audit activity, consistent with the organization's goals.

Interpretation:

To develop the risk-based plan, the chief audit executive consults with senior management and the board and obtains an understanding of the organization's strategies, key business objectives, associated risks, and risk management processes. The chief audit executive must review and adjust the plan, as necessary, in response to changes in the organization's business, risks, operations, programs, systems, and controls.

> **2010.A1** – The internal audit activity's plan of engagements must be based on a documented risk assessment, undertaken at least annually. The input of senior management and the board must be considered in this process.

2010.A2 – The chief audit executive must identify and consider the expectations of senior management, the board, and other stakeholders for internal audit opinions and other conclusions.

2010.C1 – The chief audit executive should consider accepting proposed consulting engagements based on the engagement's potential to improve management of risks, add value, and improve the organization's operations. Accepted engagements must be included in the plan.

2020—Communication and Approval

The chief audit executive must communicate the internal audit activity's plans and resource requirements, including significant interim changes, to senior management and the board for review and approval. The chief audit executive must also communicate the impact of resource limitations.

2030—Resource Management

The chief audit executive must ensure that internal audit resources are appropriate, sufficient, and effectively deployed to achieve the approved plan.

Interpretation:

Appropriate refers to the mix of knowledge, skills, and other competencies needed to perform the plan. Sufficient refers to the quantity of resources needed to accomplish the plan. Resources are effectively deployed when they are used in a way that optimizes the achievement of the approved plan.

2040—Policies and Procedures

The chief audit executive must establish policies and procedures to guide the internal audit activity.

Interpretation:

The form and content of policies and procedures are dependent upon the size and structure of the internal audit activity and the complexity of its work.

2050—Coordination and Reliance

The chief audit executive should share information, coordinate activities, and consider relying upon the work of other internal and external assurance and consulting service providers to ensure proper coverage and minimize duplication of efforts.

Interpretation:

In coordinating activities, the chief audit executive may rely on the work of other assurance and consulting service providers. A consistent process for the basis of reliance should be established, and the chief audit executive should consider the competency, objectivity, and due professional care of the assurance and consulting service providers. The chief audit executive should also have a clear understanding of the scope, objectives, and results of the work performed by other providers of assurance and consulting services. Where reliance is placed on the work of others, the chief audit executive is still accountable and responsible for ensuring adequate support for conclusions and opinions reached by the internal audit activity.

2060—Reporting to Senior Management and the Board

The chief audit executive must report periodically to senior management and the board on the internal audit activity's purpose, authority, responsibility, and performance relative to its plan and on its conformance with the Code of Ethics and the *Standards*. Reporting must also include significant risk and control issues, including fraud risks, governance issues, and other matters that require the attention of senior management and/or the board.

Interpretation:

The frequency and content of reporting are determined collaboratively by the chief audit executive, senior management, and the board. The frequency and content of reporting depends on the importance of the information to be communicated and the urgency of the related actions to be taken by senior management and/or the board.

The chief audit executive's reporting and communication to senior management and the board must include information about:

- *The audit charter.*
- *Independence of the internal audit activity.*
- *The audit plan and progress against the plan.*
- *Resource requirements.*
- *Results of audit activities.*
- *Conformance with the Code of Ethics and the* Standards, *and action plans to address any significant conformance issues.*
- *Management's response to risk that, in the chief audit executive's judgment, may be unacceptable to the organization.*

These and other chief audit executive communication requirements are referenced throughout the Standards.

2070—External Service Provider and Organizational Responsibility for Internal Auditing

When an external service provider serves as the internal audit activity, the provider must make the organization aware that the organization has the responsibility for maintaining an effective internal audit activity.

Interpretation:

This responsibility is demonstrated through the quality assurance and improvement program which assesses conformance with the Code of Ethics and the Standards.

2100—Nature of Work

The internal audit activity must evaluate and contribute to the improvement of the organization's governance, risk management, and control processes using a systematic, disciplined, and risk-based approach. Internal audit credibility and value are enhanced when auditors are proactive and their evaluations offer new insights and consider future impact.

2110—Governance

The internal audit activity must assess and make appropriate recommendations to improve the organization's governance processes for:

- Making strategic and operational decisions.
- Overseeing risk management and control.
- Promoting appropriate ethics and values within the organization.
- Ensuring effective organizational performance management and accountability.
- Communicating risk and control information to appropriate areas of the organization.
- Coordinating the activities of, and communicating information among, the board, external and internal auditors, other assurance providers, and management.

2110.A1 – The internal audit activity must evaluate the design, implementation, and effectiveness of the organization's ethics-related objectives, programs, and activities.

2110.A2 – The internal audit activity must assess whether the information technology governance of the organization supports the organization's strategies and objectives.

2120—Risk Management

The internal audit activity must evaluate the effectiveness and contribute to the improvement of risk management processes.

Interpretation:

Determining whether risk management processes are effective is a judgment resulting from the internal auditor's assessment that:

- *Organizational objectives support and align with the organization's mission.*
- *Significant risks are identified and assessed.*
- *Appropriate risk responses are selected that align risks with the organization's risk appetite.*
- *Relevant risk information is captured and communicated in a timely manner across the organization, enabling staff, management, and the board to carry out their responsibilities.*

The internal audit activity may gather the information to support this assessment during multiple engagements. The results of these engagements, when viewed together, provide an understanding of the organization's risk management processes and their effectiveness.

Risk management processes are monitored through ongoing management activities, separate evaluations, or both.

2120.A1 – The internal audit activity must evaluate risk exposures relating to the organization's governance, operations, and information systems regarding the:

- Achievement of the organization's strategic objectives.
- Reliability and integrity of financial and operational information.
- Effectiveness and efficiency of operations and programs.
- Safeguarding of assets.
- Compliance with laws, regulations, policies, procedures, and contracts.

2120.A2 – The internal audit activity must evaluate the potential for the occurrence of fraud and how the organization manages fraud risk.

2120.C1 – During consulting engagements, internal auditors must address risk consistent with the engagement's objectives and be alert to the existence of other significant risks.

2120.C2 – Internal auditors must incorporate knowledge of risks gained from consulting engagements into their evaluation of the organization's risk management processes.

2120.C3 – When assisting management in establishing or improving risk management processes, internal auditors must refrain from assuming any management responsibility by actually managing risks.

2130—Control

The internal audit activity must assist the organization in maintaining effective controls by evaluating their effectiveness and efficiency and by promoting continuous improvement.

2130.A1 – The internal audit activity must evaluate the adequacy and effectiveness of controls in responding to risks within the organization's governance, operations, and information systems regarding the:

- Achievement of the organization's strategic objectives.
- Reliability and integrity of financial and operational information.
- Effectiveness and efficiency of operations and programs.
- Safeguarding of assets.
- Compliance with laws, regulations, policies, procedures, and contracts.

2130.C1 – Internal auditors must incorporate knowledge of controls gained from consulting engagements into evaluation of the organization's control processes.

2200—Engagement Planning

Internal auditors must develop and document a plan for each engagement, including the engagement's objectives, scope, timing, and resource allocations. The plan must consider the organization's strategies, objectives, and risks relevant to the engagement.

2201—Planning Considerations

In planning the engagement, internal auditors must consider:

- The strategies and objectives of the activity being reviewed and the means by which the activity controls its performance.
- The significant risks to the activity's objectives, resources, and operations and the means by which the potential impact of risk is kept to an acceptable level.
- The adequacy and effectiveness of the activity's governance, risk management, and control processes compared to a relevant framework or model.
- The opportunities for making significant improvements to the activity's governance, risk management, and control processes.

2201.A1 – When planning an engagement for parties outside the organization, internal auditors must establish a written understanding with them about objectives, scope, respective responsibilities, and other expectations, including restrictions on distribution of the results of the engagement and access to engagement records.

2201.C1 – Internal auditors must establish an understanding with consulting engagement clients about objectives, scope, respective responsibilities, and other client expectations. For significant engagements, this understanding must be documented.

2210—Engagement Objectives

Objectives must be established for each engagement.

2210.A1 – Internal auditors must conduct a preliminary assessment of the risks relevant to the activity under review. Engagement objectives must reflect the results of this assessment.

2210.A2 – Internal auditors must consider the probability of significant errors, fraud, noncompliance, and other exposures when developing the engagement objectives.

2210.A3 – Adequate criteria are needed to evaluate governance, risk management, and controls. Internal auditors must ascertain the extent to which management and/or the board has established adequate criteria to determine whether objectives and goals have been accomplished. If adequate, internal auditors must use such criteria in their evaluation. If inadequate, internal auditors must identify appropriate evaluation criteria through discussion with management and/or the board.

Interpretation:

Types of criteria may include:

- *Internal (e.g., policies and procedures of the organization).*
- *External (e.g., laws and regulations imposed by statutory bodies).*
- *Leading practices (e.g., industry and professional guidance).*

2210.C1 – Consulting engagement objectives must address governance, risk management, and control processes to the extent agreed upon with the client.

2210.C2 – Consulting engagement objectives must be consistent with the organization's values, strategies, and objectives.

2220—Engagement Scope

The established scope must be sufficient to achieve the objectives of the engagement.

2220.A1 – The scope of the engagement must include consideration of relevant systems, records, personnel, and physical properties, including those under the control of third parties.

2220.A2 – If significant consulting opportunities arise during an assurance engagement, a specific written understanding as to the objectives, scope, respective responsibilities, and other expectations should be reached and the results of the consulting engagement communicated in accordance with consulting standards.

2220.C1 – In performing consulting engagements, internal auditors must ensure that the scope of the engagement is sufficient to address the agreed-upon objectives. If internal auditors develop reservations about the scope during the engagement, these reservations must be discussed with the client to determine whether to continue with the engagement.

2220.C2 – During consulting engagements, internal auditors must address controls consistent with the engagement's objectives and be alert to significant control issues.

2230—Engagement Resource Allocation

Internal auditors must determine appropriate and sufficient resources to achieve engagement objectives based on an evaluation of the nature and complexity of each engagement, time constraints, and available resources.

Interpretation:

Appropriate refers to the mix of knowledge, skills, and other competencies needed to perform the engagement. Sufficient refers to the quantity of resources needed to accomplish the engagement with due professional care.

2240—Engagement Work Program

Internal auditors must develop and document work programs that achieve the engagement objectives.

> **2240.A1** – Work programs must include the procedures for identifying, analyzing, evaluating, and documenting information during the engagement. The work program must be approved prior to its implementation, and any adjustments approved promptly.
>
> **2240.C1** – Work programs for consulting engagements may vary in form and content depending upon the nature of the engagement.

2300—Performing the Engagement

Internal auditors must identify, analyze, evaluate, and document sufficient information to achieve the engagement's objectives.

2310—Identifying Information

Internal auditors must identify sufficient, reliable, relevant, and useful information to achieve the engagement's objectives.

Interpretation:

Sufficient information is factual, adequate, and convincing so that a prudent, informed person would reach the same conclusions as the auditor. Reliable information is the best attainable information through the use of appropriate engagement techniques. Relevant information supports engagement observations and recommendations and is consistent with the objectives for the engagement. Useful information helps the organization meet its goals.

2320—Analysis and Evaluation

Internal auditors must base conclusions and engagement results on appropriate analyses and evaluations.

2330—Documenting Information

Internal auditors must document sufficient, reliable, relevant, and useful information to support the engagement results and conclusions.

> **2330.A1** – The chief audit executive must control access to engagement records. The chief audit executive must obtain the approval of senior management and/or legal counsel prior to releasing such records to external parties, as appropriate.
>
> **2330.A2** – The chief audit executive must develop retention requirements for engagement records, regardless of the medium in which each record is stored. These retention requirements must be consistent with the organization's guidelines and any pertinent regulatory or other requirements.
>
> **2330.C1** – The chief audit executive must develop policies governing the custody and retention of consulting engagement records, as well as their release to internal and external parties. These policies must be consistent with the organization's guidelines and any pertinent regulatory or other requirements.

2340—Engagement Supervision

Engagements must be properly supervised to ensure objectives are achieved, quality is assured, and staff is developed.

Interpretation:

The extent of supervision required will depend on the proficiency and experience of internal auditors and the complexity of the engagement. The chief audit executive has overall responsibility for supervising the engagement, whether performed by or for the internal audit activity, but may designate appropriately experienced members of the internal audit activity to perform the review. Appropriate evidence of supervision is documented and retained.

2400—Communicating Results

Internal auditors must communicate the results of engagements.

2410—Criteria for Communicating

Communications must include the engagement's objectives, scope, and results.

2410.A1 – Final communication of engagement results must include applicable conclusions, as well as applicable recommendations and/or action plans. Where appropriate, the internal auditors' opinion should be provided. An opinion must take into account the expectations of senior management, the board, and other stakeholders and must be supported by sufficient, reliable, relevant, and useful information.

Interpretation:

Opinions at the engagement level may be ratings, conclusions, or other descriptions of the results. Such an engagement may be in relation to controls around a specific process, risk, or business unit. The formulation of such opinions requires consideration of the engagement results and their significance.

2410.A2 – Internal auditors are encouraged to acknowledge satisfactory performance in engagement communications.

2410.A3 – When releasing engagement results to parties outside the organization, the communication must include limitations on distribution and use of the results.

2410.C1 – Communication of the progress and results of consulting engagements will vary in form and content depending upon the nature of the engagement and the needs of the client.

2420—Quality of Communications

Communications must be accurate, objective, clear, concise, constructive, complete, and timely.

Interpretation:

Accurate communications are free from errors and distortions and are faithful to the underlying facts. Objective communications are fair, impartial, and unbiased and are the result of a fair-minded and balanced assessment of all relevant facts and circumstances. Clear communications are easily understood and logical, avoiding unnecessary technical language and providing all significant and relevant information. Concise communications are to the point and avoid unnecessary elaboration, superfluous detail, redundancy, and wordiness. Constructive communications are helpful to the engagement client and the organization and lead to improvements where needed. Complete communications lack nothing that is essential to the target audience and include all significant and relevant information and observations to support recommendations and conclusions. Timely communications are opportune and expedient, depending on the significance of the issue, allowing management to take appropriate corrective action.

2421—Errors and Omissions

If a final communication contains a significant error or omission, the chief audit executive must communicate corrected information to all parties who received the original communication.

2430—Use of "Conducted in Conformance with the *International Standards for the Professional Practice of Internal Auditing*"

Indicating that engagements are "conducted in conformance with the *International Standards for the Professional Practice of Internal Auditing*" is appropriate only if supported by the results of the quality assurance and improvement program.

2431—Engagement Disclosure of Nonconformance

When nonconformance with the Code of Ethics or the *Standards* impacts a specific engagement, communication of the results must disclose the:

- Principle(s) or rule(s) of conduct of the Code of Ethics or the Standard(s) with which full conformance was not achieved.
- Reason(s) for nonconformance.
- Impact of nonconformance on the engagement and the communicated engagement results.

2440—Disseminating Results

The chief audit executive must communicate results to the appropriate parties.

Interpretation:

The chief audit executive is responsible for reviewing and approving the final engagement communication before issuance and for deciding to whom and how it will be disseminated. When the chief audit executive delegates these duties, he or she retains overall responsibility.

> **2440.A1** – The chief audit executive is responsible for communicating the final results to parties who can ensure that the results are given due consideration.
>
> **2440.A2** – If not otherwise mandated by legal, statutory, or regulatory requirements, prior to releasing results to parties outside the organization the chief audit executive must:

- Assess the potential risk to the organization.
- Consult with senior management and/or legal counsel as appropriate.
- Control dissemination by restricting the use of the results.

2440.C1 – The chief audit executive is responsible for communicating the final results of consulting engagements to clients.

2440.C2 – During consulting engagements, governance, risk management, and control issues may be identified. Whenever these issues are significant to the organization, they must be communicated to senior management and the board.

2450—Overall Opinions

When an overall opinion is issued, it must take into account the strategies, objectives, and risks of the organization; and the expectations of senior management, the board, and other stakeholders. The overall opinion must be supported by sufficient, reliable, relevant, and useful information.

Interpretation:

The communication will include:

- *The scope, including the time period to which the opinion pertains.*
- *Scope limitations.*
- *Consideration of all related projects, including the reliance on other assurance providers.*
- *A summary of the information that supports the opinion.*
- *The risk or control framework or other criteria used as a basis for the overall opinion.*
- *The overall opinion, judgment, or conclusion reached.*

The reasons for an unfavorable overall opinion must be stated.

2500—Monitoring Progress

The chief audit executive must establish and maintain a system to monitor the disposition of results communicated to management.

2500.A1 – The chief audit executive must establish a follow-up process to monitor and ensure that management actions have been effectively implemented or that senior management has accepted the risk of not taking action.

2500.C1 – The internal audit activity must monitor the disposition of results of consulting engagements to the extent agreed upon with the client.

2600—Communicating the Acceptance of Risks

When the chief audit executive concludes that management has accepted a level of risk that may be unacceptable to the organization, the chief audit executive must discuss the matter with senior management. If the chief audit executive determines that the matter has not been resolved, the chief audit executive must communicate the matter to the board.

Interpretation:

The identification of risk accepted by management may be observed through an assurance or consulting engagement, monitoring progress on actions taken by management as a result of prior engagements, or other means. It is not the responsibility of the chief audit executive to resolve the risk.

Implementation Guidance

Mission | Core Principles | Definition | Standards

▶ Standard 1000 – Purpose, Authority, and Responsibility

The purpose, authority, and responsibility of the internal audit activity must be formally defined in an internal audit charter, consistent with the Mission of Internal Audit and the mandatory elements of the International Professional Practices Framework (the Core Principles for the Professional Practice of Internal Auditing, the Code of Ethics, the *Standards*, and the Definition of Internal Auditing). The chief audit executive must periodically review the internal audit charter and present it to senior management and the board for approval.

(Continued on next page)

Implementation Guidance

▶ IG1000 – Purpose, Authority, and Responsibility

Getting Started

The internal audit charter is a critical document, as it records the agreed-upon purpose, authority, and responsibility of an organization's internal audit activity. To create this document, the chief audit executive (CAE) must understand the Mission of Internal Audit and the mandatory elements of The IIA's International Professional Practices Framework (IPPF)—including the Core Principles for the Professional Practice of Internal Auditing, the Code of Ethics, the *International Standards for the Professional Practice of Internal Auditing*, and the Definition of Internal Auditing.

This understanding provides the foundation for a discussion among the CAE, senior management, and the board to mutually agree upon:

- Internal audit objectives and responsibilities.
- The expectations for the internal audit activity.
- The CAE's functional and administrative reporting lines.
- The level of authority (including access to records, physical property, and personnel) required for the internal audit activity to perform engagements and fulfill its agreed-upon objectives and responsibilities.

The CAE may need to confer with the organization's legal counsel or the board secretary regarding the preferred format for charters and how to effectively and efficiently submit the proposed internal audit charter for board approval.

Considerations for Implementation

Based on the agreed-upon elements, as noted above, the CAE (or a delegate) drafts an internal audit charter. The IIA offers a model internal audit charter that may be used as a guide. Although charters may vary by organization, they typically include the following sections:

- **Introduction**—to explain the overall role and professionalism of the internal audit activity. Relevant elements of the IPPF are often cited in the introduction.

- **Authority**—to specify the internal audit activity's full access to the records, physical property, and personnel required to perform engagements and to declare internal auditors' accountability for safeguarding assets and confidentiality.

- **Organization and reporting structure**—to document the CAE's reporting structure. The CAE should report functionally to the board and administratively to a level within the organization that allows the internal audit activity to fulfill its responsibilities (see Standard 1110—Organizational Independence). This section may delve into specific functional responsibilities, such as approving the charter and internal audit plan and hiring, compensating, and terminating the CAE. It may also describe administrative responsibilities, such as supporting information flow within the organization or approving the internal audit activity's human resource administration and budgets.

- **Independence and objectivity**—to describe the importance of internal audit independence and objectivity and how these will be maintained, such as prohibiting internal auditors from having operational responsibility or authority over areas audited.

- **Responsibilities**—to lay out major areas of ongoing responsibility, such as defining the scope of assessments, writing an internal audit plan, submitting the plan to the board for approval, performing engagements, communicating the results, providing a written engagement report, and monitoring corrective actions taken by management.

- **Quality assurance and improvement**—to describe the expectations for developing, maintaining, evaluating, and communicating the results of a

---

(Continued)

Interpretation:

The internal audit charter is a formal document that defines the internal audit activity's purpose, authority, and responsibility. The internal audit charter establishes the internal audit activity's position within the organization, including the nature of the chief audit executive's functional reporting relationship with the board; authorizes access to records, personnel, and physical properties relevant to the performance of engagements; and defines the scope of internal audit activities. Final approval of the internal audit charter resides with the board.

Mission	Core Principles	Definition	Standards

quality assurance and improvement program that covers all aspects of the internal audit activity.

- **Signatures**—to document agreement among the CAE, a designated board representative, and the individual to whom the CAE reports. This section includes the date, names, and titles of signatories.

Once drafted, the proposed internal audit charter should be discussed with senior management and the board to confirm that it accurately describes the agreed-upon role and expectations or to identify desired changes. Once the draft has been accepted, the CAE formally presents it during a board meeting to be discussed and approved. The CAE and the board may also agree on the frequency with which to review and reaffirm whether the agreement's provisions continue to enable the internal audit activity to accomplish its objectives, or whether any changes are warranted. If a question should arise in the interim, the charter may be referenced and updated as needed.

Considerations for Demonstrating Conformance

The minutes of the board meetings during which the CAE initially discusses and then formally presents the internal audit charter provide documentation of conformance. In addition, the CAE retains the approved charter. Typically, the CAE asks the board to create a standing annual agenda item to discuss, update, and approve the internal audit charter as needed. Evidence that the CAE periodically reviews the internal audit charter with senior management and the board also exists in minutes from those meetings.

IG 1010 – Recognizing Mandatory Guidance in the Internal Audit Charter

> **Standard 1010 – Recognizing Mandatory Guidance in the Internal Audit Charter**
>
> The mandatory nature of the Core Principles for the Professional Practice of Internal Auditing, the Code of Ethics, the *Standards*, and the Definition of Internal Auditing must be recognized in the internal audit charter. The chief audit executive should discuss the Mission of Internal Audit and the mandatory elements of the International Professional Practices Framework with senior management and the board.

Getting Started

Before writing or revising the internal audit charter, the chief audit executive (CAE) typically reviews The IIA's International Professional Practices Framework (IPPF) to refresh his or her understanding of the Mission of Internal Audit and the mandatory elements, including the Core Principles for the Professional Practice of Internal Auditing, the Code of Ethics, the *International Standards for the Professional Practice of Internal Auditing*, and the Definition of Internal Auditing. The CAE is required to review the internal audit charter periodically and present it to senior management and the board for approval (see Standard 1000—Purpose, Authority, and Responsibility). It is helpful if the CAE knows the organization's process for submitting the internal audit charter for approval. The CAE may also arrange a discussion of the charter with senior management and the board as part of the periodic review and revision process.

Considerations for Implementation

To recognize the mandatory elements of the IPPF in the internal audit charter, the CAE may make specific statements. One example is:

"The internal audit activity will govern itself by adherence to The Institute of Internal Auditors' Mandatory Guidance, which includes the Core Principles for the Professional Practice of Internal Auditing, the Code of Ethics, the International Standards for the Professional Practice of Internal Auditing, and the Definition of Internal Auditing. The IIA's Mandatory Guidance constitutes the fundamental requirements for the professional practice of internal auditing and the principles against which to evaluate the effectiveness of the internal audit activity's performance."

An alternative to using any specific wording is to use language and content throughout the internal audit charter that require conformance with the Mandatory Guidance.

The CAE's discussion of the internal audit charter with senior management and the board provides a good opportunity to explain the Mission of Internal Audit and the mandatory elements of the IPPF, as well as how the charter recognizes those elements. After the charter has been adopted, it is important for the CAE to monitor The IIA's Mandatory Guidance and to discuss any changes that may be warranted during the next charter review.

Considerations for Demonstrating Conformance

Conformance with Standard 1010 is evidenced in the written and approved internal audit charter that recognizes the Core Principles for the Professional Practice of Internal Auditing, the Code of Ethics, the *Standards*, and Definition of Internal Auditing as mandatory elements. Conformance may also be demonstrated through the minutes of meetings during which these mandatory elements and the Mission of Internal Audit were discussed with senior management and the board. This may also include minutes from meetings during which the CAE discussed periodic reviews of the charter.

IG1100 – Independence and Objectivity

Getting Started

Independence is defined as, "The freedom from conditions that threaten the ability of the internal audit activity to carry out internal audit responsibilities in an unbiased manner." Often, such conditions stem from the organizational placement and assigned responsibilities of internal audit. For example, when internal audit reports within other functions in an organization, it is not considered independent of that function, which is subject to audit. Similarly, if the chief audit executive (CAE) has functional responsibilities broader than internal audit, such as risk management or compliance, internal audit is not independent of these additional functions, which are also subject to audit.

However, the CAE cannot solely determine the organizational independence and placement for internal audit; the CAE needs help from the board and senior management to address independence effectively. Typically, the CAE, the board, and senior management reach a shared understanding of internal audit's responsibility, authority, and expectations, which lays the groundwork for a discussion on independence and organizational placement.

Depending on board and senior management experience and expectations, reaching a common vision may require numerous discussions to increase the awareness of senior management and the board on the importance of independence, the means of achieving it, and key considerations such as reporting lines, professional and regulatory requirements, benchmarking, and organization's cultural issues.

Generally, the internal audit charter will reflect the decisions reached regarding internal audit's responsibility, authority, and expectations, as well as organizational placement and reporting lines.

Objectivity refers to an unbiased mental attitude of internal auditors. To implement this standard, the CAE will want to understand policies or activities within the organization and within internal audit that could enhance or hinder

---

▶ Standard 1100 – Independence and Objectivity

The internal audit activity must be independent, and internal auditors must be objective in performing their work.

Interpretation:

Independence is the freedom from conditions that threaten the ability of the internal audit activity to carry out internal audit responsibilities in an unbiased manner. To achieve the degree of independence necessary to effectively carry out the responsibilities of the internal audit activity, the chief audit executive has direct and unrestricted access to senior management and the board. This can be achieved through a dual-reporting relationship. Threats to independence must be managed at the individual auditor, engagement, functional, and organizational levels.

Objectivity is an unbiased mental attitude that allows internal auditors to perform engagements in such a manner that they believe in their work product and that no

(Continued on next page)

> (Continued)
>
> *quality compromises are made. Objectivity requires that internal auditors do not subordinate their judgment on audit matters to others. Threats to objectivity must be managed at the individual auditor, engagement, functional, and organizational levels.*

such a mindset. For example, many organizations have standard performance evaluation and compensation policies, as well as employee conflict of interest policies. The CAE will want to understand the nature of relevant policies identified and consider their potential impact on internal audit objectivity. Internal audit will often customize these organizationwide policies to address internal audit roles specifically and may develop other relevant policies specifically for internal audit, such as policies pertaining to training requirements.

Considerations for Implementation

As noted above, the CAE works with the board and senior management to avoid conditions that would affect internal audit's ability to perform its responsibilities in an unbiased manner. Often, the CAE has a direct functional reporting line to the board and an administrative reporting line to a member of senior management. The reporting line to the board provides the CAE with direct board access for sensitive matters and enables sufficient organizational status. Administrative reporting to a member of senior management also provides the CAE with sufficient organizational status, as well as authority to perform duties without impediment and to address difficult issues with other senior leaders. For example, the CAE would not typically report to a controller or mid-level manager, who may be subject to audit routinely.

The IIA recommends that the CAE report administratively to the chief executive officer (CEO), both so that the CAE is clearly a senior position and so that internal audit is not positioned within an operation that is subject to audit. The CAE should also be aware of any requirements from regulators or other governing bodies that may specify a required reporting relationship. The Implementation Guide for Standard 1110—Organizational Independence provides further guidance on CAE reporting relationships.

It is also recommended that the CAE not have operational responsibilities beyond internal audit, as these other responsibilities may, themselves, be subject to audit. In some organizations, the CAE is asked to assume operational responsibilities, such as for risk management or compliance. In such situations, the CAE typically discusses the independence concerns and the potential objectivity impairment with the board and senior management, who will implement safeguards to limit the impairment. Safeguards are oversight activities, generally undertaken by the board, to monitor and address independence conflicts. Examples include periodically evaluating CAE responsibilities, developing alternate processes to obtain assurance related to the additional areas of responsibility, and being aware of the potential objectivity impairment when considering internal audit risk assessments.

To manage internal audit objectivity effectively, many CAEs have an internal audit policy manual or handbook that describes expectations and requirements for an unbiased mindset. Such a policy manual may describe:

- The critical importance of objectivity to the internal audit profession.
- Typical situations that could undermine objectivity, due to self-interest, self-review, familiarity, bias, and undue influence. Examples include auditing in an area where an internal auditor recently worked; auditing a family member or a close friend; or assuming, without evidence that an area under audit is acceptable based solely on prior positive experiences.
- Actions the internal auditor should take if he or she becomes aware of a current or potential objectivity concern, such as discussing the concern with an internal audit manager or the CAE.
- Reporting requirements where each internal auditor periodically considers and discloses conflicts of interest.

To reinforce the importance of these policies and help ensure all internal auditors internalize their importance, some CAEs will hold routine workshops or training on these fundamental concepts. Such training sessions will often allow internal auditors to better understand objectivity by considering objectivity-impairing scenarios and how best to address them. Further, when assigning internal auditors to specific engagements, the CAE will consider potential objectivity impairments and avoid assigning team members who may have a conflict.

It is widely understood that performance and compensation practices can significantly and negatively affect an individual's objectivity. For example, if an internal auditor's performance evaluation, salary, or bonus are significantly based on client satisfaction surveys, the internal auditor may hesitate to report negative results that may cause the client to report low satisfaction ratings. Therefore, the CAE needs to be thoughtful in designing the internal audit performance evaluation and compensation system and consider whether the measurements used could impair an internal auditor's objectivity. Ideally, the evaluation process will balance internal auditor performance, audit results, and client feedback measurements. The Implementation Guide for Standard 1120—Individual Objectivity provides further guidance on objectivity.

Considerations for Demonstrating Conformance

Multiple items may indicate conformance with the standard, including the internal audit charter itself; an organization chart with reporting responsibilities; an internal audit policy manual that includes policies on independence, objectivity, addressing conflicts, and performance evaluation; training records; and conflict-of-interest disclosure forms. If applicable, documentation showing disclosure of impairments, consistent with Standard 1130—Impairment to Independence or Objectivity, may also demonstrate conformanc

▶ IG 1110 – Organizational Independence

Getting Started

The standard requires the chief audit executive (CAE) to report to a level within the organization that allows internal audit to fulfill its responsibilities. Therefore, it is necessary to consider the organizational placement and supervisory oversight/reporting lines of internal audit to ensure organizational independence.

The CAE does not solely determine the organizational placement of internal audit, the CAE's reporting relationships, or the nature of board or senior management supervision; the CAE needs help from the board and senior management to address these items effectively. Typically, the CAE, the board, and senior management reach a shared understanding of internal audit's responsibility, authority, and expectations, as well as the role of the board and senior management in overseeing internal audit. Generally, the internal audit charter documents the decisions reached on organizational placement and reporting lines.

It may also be helpful for the CAE to be aware of regulatory requirements for both internal audit positioning and CAE reporting lines.

Considerations for Implementation

As noted above, the CAE works with the board and senior management to determine organizational placement of internal audit, including the CAE's reporting relationships. To ensure effective organizational independence, the CAE has a direct functional reporting line to the board. Generally, the CAE also has an administrative, or "dotted," reporting line to a member of senior management.

A functional reporting line to the board provides the CAE with direct board access for sensitive matters and enables sufficient organizational status. It ensures that the CAE has unrestricted access to the board, typically the highest level of governance in the organization.

▶ Standard 1110 – Organizational Independence

The chief audit executive must report to a level within the organization that allows the internal audit activity to fulfill its responsibilities. The chief audit executive must confirm to the board, at least annually, the organizational independence of the internal audit activity.

Interpretation:

Organizational independence is effectively achieved when the chief audit executive reports functionally to the board. Examples of functional reporting to the board involve the board:

- *Approving the internal audit charter.*
- *Approving the risk-based internal audit plan.*
- *Approving the internal audit budget and resource plan.*
- *Receiving communications from the chief audit executive on the internal audit activity's performance relative to its plan and other matters.*

(Continued on next page)

| Mission | Core Principles | Definition | Standards |

> (Continued)
>
> - *Approving decisions regarding the appointment and removal of the chief audit executive.*
> - *Approving the remuneration of the chief audit executive.*
> - *Making appropriate inquiries of management and the chief audit executive to determine whether there are inappropriate scope or resource limitations.*

Functional oversight requires the board to create the right working conditions to permit the operation of an independent and effective internal audit activity. As noted, the board assumes responsibility for approving the internal audit charter, the internal audit plan, the budget and resource plan, the evaluation and compensation of the CAE, and the appointment and removal of the CAE. Further, the board monitors the ability of internal audit to operate independently. It does so by asking the CAE and members of management questions regarding internal audit scope, resource limitations, or other pressures or hindrances on internal audit.

CAEs who find themselves with a board that does not assume these important functional oversight duties may share Standard 1110 and recommended governance practices—including board responsibilities—with the board to pursue a stronger functional relationship over time.

To facilitate board oversight, the CAE routinely provides the board with performance updates, generally at quarterly meetings of the board. Often, the CAE is involved in crafting board meeting agendas and can plan for sufficient time to discuss internal audit performance relative to plan as well as other matters, including key findings or emerging risks that warrant the board's attention. Further, to ensure that organizational independence is discussed annually, as required by this standard, the CAE will often create a standing board agenda item for a specific board meeting each year.

Generally, the CAE also has an administrative reporting line to senior management, which further enables the requisite stature and authority of internal audit to fulfill responsibilities. For example, the CAE typically would not report to a controller, accounting manager, or mid-level functional manager. To enhance stature and credibility, The IIA recommends that the CAE report administratively to the chief executive officer (CEO) so that the CAE is clearly in a senior position, with the authority to perform duties unimpeded.

Considerations for Demonstrating Conformance

There are several documents that may demonstrate conformance with this standard, including the internal audit charter and the audit committee charter, which would describe the audit committee's oversight duties. The CAE's job description and performance evaluation would note reporting relationships and supervisory oversight. If available, CAE hiring documentation may include who interviewed the CAE and who made the hiring decision. Further, an internal audit policy manual that addresses policies like independence and board communication requirements or an organization chart with reporting responsibilities may demonstrate conformance. Board reports, meeting minutes, and agendas can demonstrate that internal audit has appropriately communicated items such as the internal audit plan, budget, and performance, as well as the state of organizational independence.

| Mission | Core Principles | Definition | Standards |

> **Standard 1111 – Direct Interaction with the Board**
>
> The chief audit executive must communicate and interact directly with the board.

▶ IG1111 – Direct Interaction with the Board

Getting Started

Generally, the chief audit executive (CAE), the board, and senior management have discussed and agreed on internal audit's responsibility, authority, and expectations as well as the necessary organizational placement of internal audit and CAE reporting relationships to enable internal audit to fulfill its duties. The reporting relationship typically includes a direct functional reporting relationship with the board. Refer to Implementation Guides 1100—Independence and Objectivity and Implementation Guide 1110—Organizational Independence for additional guidance.

Considerations for Implementation

If the CAE has a direct functional reporting relationship with the board, then the board assumes responsibility for approving the internal audit charter, internal audit plan, internal audit budget and resource plan, evaluation and compensation of the CAE, and appointment and removal of the CAE. Further, the board monitors the ability of internal audit to operate independently and fulfill its charter.

With such a reporting relationship, the CAE will have many opportunities to communicate and interact directly with the board, as required by this standard. For example, the CAE will participate in audit committee and/or full board meetings, generally quarterly, to communicate such things as the proposed internal audit plan, budget, progress, and any challenges. Further, the CAE will have the ability to contact the chair or any member of the board to communicate sensitive matters or issues facing internal audit or the organization. Typically, and at least annually, a private meeting with the board or audit committee and the CAE (without senior management present) is formally conducted to discuss such matters or issues. It is also helpful for the CAE to participate in one-on-one meetings or phone calls periodically with the board or audit committee chair, either prior to scheduled meetings or routinely during the year, to ensure direct and open communication.

CAEs who find themselves without direct access to the board can share Standard 1111 (as well as standards 1100 and 1110), recommended governance practices, and board/audit committee best practice studies to pursue a stronger relationship and direct access. Further, CAEs in such a situation can consider written communications to the board until a direct line of communication, as required by this standard, is available.

Considerations for Demonstrating Conformance

Board meeting agendas and minutes are often sufficient to demonstrate whether the CAE has communicated and interacted directly with the board. The CAE's calendar may also demonstrate conformance. Further, a policy that requires the CAE to meet privately with the board periodically may be documented in board or audit committee charters.

| Mission | Core Principles | Definition | Standards |

▶ Standard 1112 – Chief Audit Executive Roles Beyond Internal Auditing

Where the chief audit executive has or is expected to have roles and/or responsibilities that fall outside of internal auditing, safeguards must be in place to limit impairments to independence or objectivity.

Interpretation:

The chief audit executive may be asked to take on additional roles and responsibilities outside of internal auditing, such as responsibility for compliance or risk management activities. These roles and responsibilities may impair, or appear to impair, the organizational independence of the internal audit activity or the individual objectivity of the internal auditor. Safeguards are those oversight activities, often undertaken by the board, to address these potential impairments, and may include such activities as periodically evaluating reporting lines and responsibilities and developing alternative processes to obtain assurance related to the areas of additional responsibility.

▶ IG1112 – Chief Audit Executive Roles Beyond Internal Auditing

Getting Started

The Interpretation of Standard 1112 notes that when the chief audit executive (CAE) takes on roles and/or responsibilities outside of internal auditing, organizational independence of the internal audit activity or the individual objectivity of the internal auditor may be impaired or may appear to be impaired. However, in certain circumstances, the board and senior management may find that it is appropriate for the organization to expand the CAE's role beyond internal auditing.

Examples of situations when the CAE may be asked to perform roles for which management is normally responsible include:

- A new regulatory requirement prompts a pressing need to develop policies, procedures, controls, and risk management activities to ensure compliance.
- An organization needs current risk management activities to be adapted for the addition of a new business segment or geographical market.
- The organization's resources are too constrained, or the organization is too small, to afford a separate compliance function.
- The organization's processes are immature, and the CAE has the most appropriate expertise to introduce risk management principles in the organization.

In some cases, the CAE may be expected to assume responsibilities in the areas of risk management, design and operation of controls, and compliance. For example, if a CAE is asked to take on a role that reports functionally to senior management instead of the board, the CAE's independence related to internal audit responsibilities may be impaired. (See Implementation Guide 1130 – Impairment to Independence or Objectivity for additional examples of potential impairments.) Standard 1112 guides the CAE in such cases.

To implement Standard 1112, the CAE must have a clear understanding of The IIA's

Code of Ethics and the concepts of independence and objectivity, as explained in the 1100 series of standards and implementation guides. Additionally, several of The IIA's Core Principles for the Professional Practice of Internal Auditing address independence and objectivity of the CAE. The internal audit activity's mission statement and charter, the audit committee charter, and the organization's policies and code of ethics may include additional relevant guidance specific to the organization.

To address the risks of impairment, the CAE should gain an understanding of any proposed role that falls outside of internal auditing and speak with senior management and the board about the reporting relationships, responsibilities, and expectations related to the role. During such a discussion, the CAE should emphasize the IIA standards related to independence and objectivity, the potential impairment presented by the proposed role, the risks associated with the proposed role, and safeguards that could mitigate those risks.

Considerations for Implementation

Standard 1112 emphasizes the importance of safeguards such as oversight activities, often undertaken by the board, to address potential impairments to the CAE's independence and objectivity. One safeguard is the CAE's organizational position and reporting relationship. According to Standard 1110 – Organizational Independence, "The CAE must report to a level within the organization that allows the internal audit activity to fulfill its responsibilities." This is effectively achieved when the CAE reports functionally to the board, which usually involves board oversight of the hiring, evaluation, and compensation of the CAE and board approval of the internal audit charter and internal audit plan, budget, and resources. As stated in Standard 1000 – Purpose, Authority, and Responsibility, the internal audit charter documents the nature of the CAE's functional reporting relationship with the board.

Changes in the organization and its key personnel may lead to the repositioning or redefinition of roles and responsibilities. According to the Interpretation of Standard 1112, one safeguard that may address this situation is the periodic evaluation of reporting lines and responsibilities. The CAE's review of the internal audit charter and discussion with senior management and the board, as described in Standard 1000, should include any changes in roles or responsibilities that may affect the internal audit activity, particularly those that have the potential to impair the CAE's independence and objectivity, either in fact or appearance. If the CAE's nonaudit responsibilities will be ongoing, the internal audit charter should describe the nature of the work. However, if such responsibilities will be short-term, changes to the internal audit charter and other documents may not be necessary. In such cases, a plan to transition these responsibilities to management may be implemented to safeguard the CAE's independence and objectivity. The transition plan would ensure the proper resources and timeline to facilitate management's acceptance of these responsibilities.

Standard 1130 requires the CAE to disclose the details of any impairment to independence or objectivity, whether in fact or appearance. Disclosures, which enable the board to evaluate the overall risk of potential impairments, typically take place during a board meeting and may include a discussion of related topics, such as:

- Roles and responsibilities that the CAE is being asked to undertake.
- Risks related to the undertaking.
- Safeguards to the CAE's independence and objectivity, including consideration of appearances.
- Controls in place to validate that the safeguards are operating effectively.
- Transition plan, if the assignment is short-term.
- Agreement with senior management and the board.

The board can monitor the CAE's objectivity by increasing the level of scrutiny applied to the CAE's risk assessment, internal audit plan, and engagement communications, and considering any potential bias the CAE may have related to an area for which he or she performed duties beyond internal auditing. To help safeguard the CAE from impairments to objectivity, Standard 1130.A1 prohibits internal auditors from assessing specific operations for which they were responsible within the previous year, and Standard 1130.A2 requires a party outside the internal audit activity to oversee assurance engagements for functions over which the CAE has responsibility. If the CAE has responsibilities in areas outside the internal audit activity that are subject to internal auditing, the provision of assurance would be outsourced to an objective, competent assurance provider that reports independently to the board, rather than the CAE. Such an assurance provider could be either internal or external.

An external assessment of the internal audit activity (see Standard 1312 – External Assessments) that includes a review of the CAE's independence and objectivity—particularly in areas where the CAE has executed nonaudit responsibilities can provide additional assurance to the board, as long as the independence of the external assessor can be validated.

Considerations for Demonstrating Conformance

Documentation of any safeguards that were established to address potential impairments to the CAE's independence and objectivity may help demonstrate conformance with Standard 1112. Such documentation may include statements in the organization's policies and code of ethics, the audit committee's charter, and the internal audit activity's mission statement and approved audit charter, which specifies the CAE's roles and responsibilities as agreed with senior management and the board. Conformance may also be demonstrated through periodic revisions of the internal audit charter, which reflect the internal audit activity's changing roles and responsibilities. Likewise, plans to transition roles and responsibilities that fall outside of internal auditing (e.g., compliance or risk management activities) from the CAE to management may also demonstrate conformance. Additional evidence could include the minutes of board meetings during which the CAE disclosed potential impairments to independence or objectivity, and proposed safeguards to mitigate the risks of impairment to acceptable levels.

The CAE could demonstrate conformance by showing that other assurance providers assessed the areas where the CAE had undertaken roles beyond internal auditing, and the internal audit plan, risk assessments, and engagement communications were independently assessed for independence and objectivity. Surveys of audit clients and board evaluations of the CAE's performance may include feedback on the perception of the CAE's independence and objectivity. Conformance may also be validated in the results of external assessments performed by an independent assessor.

| Mission | Core Principles | Definition | Standards |

▶ Standard 1120 – Individual Objectivity

Internal auditors must have an impartial, unbiased attitude and avoid any conflict of interest.

Interpretation:

Conflict of interest is a situation in which an internal auditor, who is in a position of trust, has a competing professional or personal interest. Such competing interests can make it difficult to fulfill his or her duties impartially. A conflict of interest exists even if no unethical or improper act results. A conflict of interest can create an appearance of impropriety that can undermine confidence in the internal auditor, the internal audit activity, and the profession. A conflict of interest could impair an individual's ability to perform his or her duties and responsibilities objectively.

▶ IG1120 – Individual Objectivity

Getting Started

Objectivity refers to an internal auditor's impartial and unbiased mindset, which is facilitated by avoiding conflicts of interest. Therefore, to implement this standard, the chief audit executive (CAE) will first want to understand policies or activities within the organization and within internal audit that could enhance or hinder such a mindset. For example, many organizations have standard performance evaluation and compensation policies, as well as employee conflict of interest policies. Internal audit will often customize these policies to address internal audit roles specifically and may have other relevant departmental policies, such as policies that specify training requirements. The CAE will want to understand the nature of relevant policies identified and consider their potential impact on internal audit objectivity.

Considerations for Implementation

To manage internal audit objectivity effectively, many CAEs have an internal audit policy manual or handbook that describes the expectation and requirements for an unbiased mindset for every internal auditor. Such a policy manual may describe:

- The critical importance of objectivity to the internal audit profession.

- Typical situations that could undermine objectivity, such as auditing in an area in where an internal auditor recently worked; auditing a family member or a close friend; or assuming, without evidence, that an area under audit is acceptable based solely on prior positive experiences.

- Actions the internal auditor should take if he or she becomes aware of a current or potential objectivity concern, such as discussing the concern with an internal audit manager or the CAE.

- Reporting requirements, where each internal auditor periodically considers and discloses conflicts of interest. Often, policies require internal auditors to indicate that they understand the conflict of interest policy and to disclose potential conflicts. Internal auditors sign annual statements indicating that no potential threats exist or acknowledging any known potential threats.

To reinforce the importance of these policies and help ensure all internal auditors internalize their importance, many CAEs will hold routine workshops or training on these fundamental concepts. Such training sessions will often allow internal auditors to better understand objectivity by considering objectivity-impairing scenarios and how best to address them. For example, more senior auditors and managers may share personal experiences where objectivity was called into question or where they self-disclosed a relationship or experience that was a conflict. Another common related training topic is professional skepticism. Such training reinforces the nature of skepticism and the criticality of avoiding bias and maintaining an open and curious mindset. Further, when assigning internal auditors to specific engagements, the CAE (or delegate) will consider potential objectivity impairments and avoid assigning team members who may have a conflict, as described above. For example, when internal auditors have moved into internal audit from other departments, the CAE must follow Standard 1130.A1, which requires internal auditors to refrain from assessing operations for which they were previously responsible for at least one year after leaving the operation. In addition, the CAE (or delegate) will discuss with potential team members the nature of an assignment and the individuals and departments involved, and explore whether there is a conflict that would impair (or appear to impair) an internal auditor's objectivity. Internal auditors are encouraged to share any concerns they may have so that internal audit management can determine whether the internal auditor may participate on the engagement.

It is widely understood that performance and compensation practices can significantly and negatively affect an individual's objectivity. For example, if an internal auditor's performance evaluation, salary or bonus are significantly based on client satisfaction surveys, the internal auditor may hesitate to report negative results that may cause the client to report low satisfaction ratings. Or, if the auditor evaluation process is heavily focused on the number of observations, or on staying within the audit budget, it could cause the internal auditor to lose objectivity and either report a relatively minor issue as an audit finding, or ignore warning signs of new issues that arise near the end of an engagement, when the budget is nearly depleted. Therefore, the CAE needs to be thoughtful in designing the internal audit performance evaluation and compensation system and consider whether the measurements used could impair an internal auditor's objectivity. Ideally, the evaluation process will balance auditor performance, audit results, and client feedback measurements.

Considerations for Demonstrating Conformance

Documentation that may demonstrate conformance with the standard includes the internal policy manual, which contains performance evaluation and compensation processes as well as clear policies on objectivity and avoiding and reporting conflicts of interest. Training records or materials may demonstrate that internal auditors have been made aware of the importance of objectivity, the nature of threats to objectivity, and examples of conflicts of interest.

In addition, if a related policy at the organization or internal audit level exists, there may be signed acknowledgement forms to disclose the existence (or nonexistence) of conflicts. Engagement workpapers would document the team assigned and could be compared to employment records or acknowledgement forms to confirm that known conflicts were avoided.

IG1130 – Impairment to Independence or Objectivity

Getting Started

The standard requires the chief audit executive (CAE) to disclose real or perceived impairments to independence or objectivity. Therefore, the CAE must have a clear understanding of independence and objectivity requirements, as described in the Code of Ethics and standards 1100, 1110, 1111, 1112, and 1120. Further, by communicating these requirements to the board and senior management, the CAE will help ensure that they understand the criticality of independence and objectivity for an effective internal audit activity. Generally, the board and senior management will want to discuss how and to whom impairments are disclosed, depending on the nature and potential impact of the impairment.

To fully understand and appreciate independence and objectivity, it is important that internal auditors consider the perspectives of their various stakeholders and the conditions that could be perceived as undermining (or appearing to undermine) independence or objectivity. Often, the CAE will develop an internal audit policy manual or handbook that includes a discussion of organizational independence and internal auditor objectivity, the nature of impairments, and how internal auditors should handle potential impairments.

Considerations for Implementation

As noted above, to effectively manage independence and objectivity, including impairments, many CAEs have an internal audit policy manual or handbook that describes the related expectations and requirements. In addition to defining *independence* and *objectivity*, such a manual may identify the specific related standards; describe the types of situations that could create, or appear to create, impairments; and specify the expected actions the internal auditor should undertake if faced with a potential impairment.

Impairment situations generally include self-interest, self-review, familiarity, bias, or undue influence. These situations can lead to personal conflicts of interest, scope

▶ Standard 1130 – Impairment to Independence or Objectivity

If independence or objectivity is impaired in fact or appearance, the details of the impairment must be disclosed to appropriate parties. The nature of the disclosure will depend upon the impairment.

Interpretation:

Impairment to organizational independence and individual objectivity may include, but is not limited to, personal conflict of interest; scope limitations; restrictions on access to records, personnel, and properties; and resource limitations, such as funding.

The determination of appropriate parties to which the details of an impairment to independence or objectivity must be disclosed is dependent upon the expectations of the internal audit activity's and the chief audit executive's responsibilities to senior management and the board as described in the internal audit charter, as well as the nature of the impairment.

limitations, resource limitations, or restrictions on access to records, personnel, or properties. Internal audit examples of organizational independence impairments include the following, which, if in effect, can also undermine internal auditor objectivity:

- The CAE has broader functional responsibility than internal audit and executes an audit of a functional area that is also under the CAE's oversight.
- The CAE's supervisor has broader responsibility than internal audit, and the CAE executes an audit within his or her supervisor's functional responsibility.
- The CAE does not have direct communication or interaction with the board.
- The budget for the internal audit activity is reduced to the point that internal audit cannot fulfill its responsibilities as outlined in the charter. (Standard 2020—Communication and Approval, provides further guidance on communicating the impact of resource limitations.

Examples of objectivity impairments include:

- An internal auditor audits an area in which he or she recently worked, such as when an employee transfers into internal audit from a different functional area of the organization and then is assigned to an audit of that function. (Standard 1130.A1 specifically addresses this situation).
- An internal auditor audits an area where a relative or close friend is employed.
- An internal auditor assumes, without evidence, that an area being audited has effectively mitigated risks based solely on a prior positive audit or personal experiences (e.g., a lack of professional skepticism).
- An internal auditor modifies the planned approach or results based on the undue influence of another person, often someone senior to the internal auditor, without appropriate justification.

Often, the internal audit policy manual describes the appropriate actions for an internal auditor to take should he or she become aware of, or concerned about, such impairments. Typically, the first step is to discuss the concern with an internal audit manager or the CAE to determine whether the situation is truly an impairment and how best to proceed. Both the nature of the impairment and board/senior management expectations will determine the appropriate parties to be notified of the impairment and the ideal communication approach. For example:

- When the CAE believes the impairment is not real, but recognizes there could be a *perception* of impairment, the CAE may choose to discuss the concern in engagement planning meetings with the operating management, document the discussion (such as in an audit planning memo), and explain why the concern is without merit. Such a disclosure may also be appropriate for a final engagement report.

- When the CAE believes the impairment is real and is affecting the ability of internal audit to perform its duties independently and objectively, the CAE is likely to discuss the impairment with the board and senior management and seek their support to resolve the situation.

- When an impairment comes to light after an audit has been executed, and it impacts the reliability (or perceived reliability) of the engagement results, the CAE will discuss it with operating and senior management, as well as the board. (Standard 2421—Errors and Omissions states that if a final communication contains a significant error or omission, the CAE must communicate corrected information to all parties who received the original communication.)

The CAE is usually personally involved in determining the best disclosure approach.

Considerations for Demonstrating Conformance

Multiple documents may demonstrate conformance with the standard, including an internal audit policy manual that includes policies on independence, objectivity, addressing conflicts, and the nature of impairments, and how to communicate them. Other documentation may include board meeting minutes, if impairments to independence or objectivity were discussed; memos to file; or reports that contain such disclosures.

| Mission | Core Principles | Definition | Standards |

> **Standard 1200 – Proficiency and Due Professional Care**
>
> Engagements must be performed with proficiency and due professional care.

▶ IG1200 – Proficiency and Due Professional Care

Getting Started

Performing engagements with proficiency and due professional care is the responsibility of every internal auditor. Achieving the two attributes begins with an understanding of the Mandatory Guidance of the International Professional Practices Framework (IPPF), especially The IIA's Code of Ethics.

Internal auditors usually develop proficiency via education, experience, professional development opportunities, and qualifications such as the internal audit profession's most relevant certification, the Certified Internal Auditor® (CIA®), granted by The IIA. Internal auditors who have attained professional certifications need to be aware of the continuing education requirements to keep their certifications current.

Due professional care requires understanding the IPPF's systematic and disciplined approach to internal auditing, which is supplemented by organization-specific policies and procedures established by the chief audit executive (CAE).

The CAE is responsible for ensuring conformance with this standard by the internal audit activity as a whole. As part of managing the internal audit activity, the CAE establishes policies and procedures that enable internal auditors to perform engagements with proficiency and due professional care. This involves the CAE's recruitment and training of internal auditors, as well as the proper planning, staffing, and supervising of engagements. To start, the CAE may review the responsibilities established in the internal audit charter and internal audit plan and reflect on the knowledge, skills, and other competencies that the internal audit activity will need to possess to complete the planned audit engagements.

Considerations for Implementation

For internal auditors, due professional care requires conformance with The IIA's Code of Ethics and may entail compliance to the organization's code of conduct and any additional codes of conduct relevant to other professional designations attained. Internal audit activities may have a formal process requiring an internal auditor to sign an annual declaration related to The IIA's Code of Ethics or the organization's code of conduct.

Internal auditors generally develop individual proficiency throughout their careers by obtaining and maintaining appropriate certifications, experience, and professional education, which includes continuing professional development. The CAE may use The IIA's Global Internal Audit Competency Framework or a similar benchmark to establish the criteria by which to assess the proficiency of internal auditors. The criteria may be used to create job descriptions and an inventory of the competencies needed within the internal audit activity. Additionally, the CAE may develop a strategy for recruiting, assigning, training, and professionally developing staff in order to establish a proficient internal audit activity and ensure that its competencies remain current and sufficient.

In developing the internal audit plan, the CAE generally thinks about alignment between the knowledge, skills, and other competencies needed to complete the plan and the resources available among the internal audit activity and other providers of assurance and consulting services. The CAE and internal audit supervisors may compare the skills needed to accomplish each engagement's scope and objectives with the proficiency of each available internal auditor.

To ensure due professional care is applied, the CAE must establish policies and procedures (Standard 2040), which generally incorporate the Mandatory Guidance of the IPPF and provide a systematic and disciplined approach to the engagement process. The CAE may require individual auditors to sign forms acknowledging that they understand policies and procedures.

Internal auditors can use their knowledge to assess the engagement's scope and objectives and determine how to complete the engagement effectively. By following the Mandatory Guidance of the IPPF and the internal audit policies and procedures for planning, executing, and documenting audit engagements, internal auditors are essentially exercising due professional care. Standards 1220 through

1220.A3 identify fundamental elements that internal auditors must address to demonstrate due professional care.

After engagements are completed, the CAE or engagement supervisor generally reviews the engagement process, results, and conclusions. This may be followed by a meeting with the internal audit staff that conducted the engagement to discuss relevant observations and inform a supervisory assessment of how diligently the established procedures were followed.

Considerations for Demonstrating Conformance

Evidence demonstrating conformance with Standard 1200 could include any of the following:

- Competency assessments of the internal audit activity.
- Records of a recruitment and training strategy, job descriptions, and resumes.
- Internal audit policies and procedures and workpaper templates.
- Evidence that internal audit policies and procedures were communicated and signed acknowledgement that the internal audit staff understand them.
- Evidence supporting annual declaration related to The IIA's Code of Ethics and the organization's code of conduct.
- The internal audit plan and engagement plans, which demonstrate the sufficient and appropriate allocation of internal audit staff.

Internal auditors' due professional care may be evidenced in engagement workpapers or other documentation of the procedures and processes used during the audit engagement. Documented supervisory reviews of engagements and post-engagement client surveys or other forms of feedback could indicate the proficiency and due professional care exhibited by individual internal auditors. Independent external assessments, performed as part of the quality assurance and improvement program, may provide additional assurance that engagements were performed with proficiency and due professional care.

IG1210 – Proficiency

Getting Started

To achieve this standard, it is essential that internal auditors understand and apply the Mandatory Guidance of The IIA's International Professional Practices Framework (IPPF) and have certain knowledge, skills, and competencies. Ensuring the collective proficiency of the internal audit activity is the overall responsibility of the chief audit executive (CAE), who must effectively manage the internal audit activity and its resources to accomplish the internal audit plan and add value to the organization. (The 2000 series of standards addresses the details of managing the internal audit activity and internal audit resources.)

The IIA's Global Internal Audit Competency Framework defines the core competencies needed to fulfill IPPF requirements for all occupational levels of the internal audit profession, including staff, management, and executive. To conform with Standard 1210, the CAE and internal auditors may want to review, understand, and reflect on the competencies that comprise the Competency Framework.

Considerations for Implementation

To build and maintain the proficiency of the internal audit activity, the CAE may develop a competency assessment tool or skills assessment based on the Competency Framework or another benchmark (e.g., a mature internal audit activity). Then, the CAE could incorporate the basic criteria of internal audit competency into job descriptions and recruitment material to help attract and hire internal auditors with the appropriate educational background and experience. The CAE may also use the competency assessment tool to complete a periodic skills assessment of the internal audit activity to identify gaps. When doing so, the CAE should consider risks related to fraud and IT, as well as available technology-based audit techniques, as required by standards 1210.A2 and 1210.A3.

Standard 1210 – Proficiency

Internal auditors must possess the knowledge, skills, and other competencies needed to perform their individual responsibilities. The internal audit activity collectively must possess or obtain the knowledge, skills, and other competencies needed to perform its responsibilities.

Interpretation:

Proficiency is a collective term that refers to the knowledge, skills, and other competencies required of internal auditors to effectively carry out their professional responsibilities. It encompasses consideration of current activities, trends, and emerging issues, to enable relevant advice and recommendations. Internal auditors are encouraged to demonstrate their proficiency by obtaining appropriate professional certifications and qualifications, such as the Certified Internal Auditor designation and other designations offered by The Institute of Internal Auditors and other appropriate professional organizations.

The CAE has additional obligations related to ensuring the collective proficiency of the internal audit activity. These include managing the internal audit activity in conformance with the Mandatory Guidance of the IPPF (Standard 2000—Managing the Internal Audit Activity) and ensuring that the internal audit activity has the appropriate mix of knowledge, skills, and other competencies to fulfill the internal audit plan (Standard 2030—Resource Management). If the internal audit activity does not have appropriate and sufficient resources on staff, the CAE is expected to obtain competent advice or assistance to fill any gaps. The CAE can use the criteria defined in the Competency Framework to identify gaps in the internal audit activity's collective proficiency and to develop plans for filling coverage gaps through hiring, training, outsourcing, and other methods. (Standard 2050 and its respective implementation guide address the details of coordinating activities with other internal and external providers of assurance and consulting services.)

To enhance proficiency of the internal audit activity, the CAE would encourage professional development of internal auditors, whether that occurs through on-the-job training, attendance at professional conferences and seminars, or encouraging the pursuit of professional certifications. By regularly reviewing the performance of internal auditors, the CAE may gain insight into training needs and provide feedback to help develop individuals.

This standard also requires individual internal auditors to possess the knowledge, skills, and competencies needed to carry out their responsibilities effectively. Individuals may use the Competency Framework as a basis for self-assessment. Moreover, the standard encourages internal auditors to obtain appropriate certifications and qualifications to further support professional growth and increased proficiency for both the individual and the internal audit activity as a whole. Likewise, Standard 1230—Continuing Professional Development requires internal auditors to enhance their competencies through continuing professional development. Internal auditors should keep themselves informed about the continuing education that may be required to maintain any professional certifications they hold.

Because Standard 1210 requires proficiency that encompasses consideration of current activities, trends, and emerging issues, continuing education could include opportunities to learn about changes in the industry that may affect the organization or the internal audit profession. The CAE may help ensure the internal audit activity's overall proficiency in this regard. For example, the CAE could subscribe to industry news services or emailed newsletters, which are likely to include information about recently published studies and white papers. The CAE may also attend or recommend to the audit staff online or in-person seminars. Periodically, the CAE may schedule internal staff training events to introduce new technology or changes in internal audit practices.

At the level of the individual engagement, the CAE assumes overall responsibility for supervising the engagement to ensure quality, achievement of objectives, and staff development (Standard 2340—Engagement Supervision). The proficiency and experience of internal auditors help determine the extent of supervision required. To stay informed, the CAE may periodically reassess the skills of individual internal auditors. Also, as an engagement is completed, the CAE or an engagement supervisor may survey and/or interview the engagement client (formally or informally) to solicit feedback about the internal auditor's proficiency in performing the engagement.

The individual responsibilities of internal auditors at the level of engagement planning include considering the appropriateness and sufficiency of resources to achieve engagement objectives (Standard 2230—Engagement Resource Allocation). Internal auditors usually review the objectives and scope of audit engagements and then discuss with the CAE any limitations in their competencies that might prevent them from achieving those engagement objectives.

Considerations for Demonstrating Conformance

Individual internal auditors may evidence their proficiency through their resumes or curriculum vitae and by maintaining records of certifications and continuing professional development (e.g., courses for continuing education credits; participation in conferences, workshops, and seminars; performance reviews).

The CAE's effort to establish and maintain a proficient internal audit activity may be demonstrated through the use of a competency assessment tool and the development of internal audit policies, procedures, and training materials. Efforts to recruit and hire proficient internal auditors may be reflected in job descriptions and other recruitment materials.

The CAE or an audit engagement supervisor may retain records of their evaluation of individual internal auditors and the internal audit activity as a whole. Such evaluations may include individual performance reviews and post-engagement discussions, memos, and meeting minutes. Documented feedback from post-engagement client surveys and interviews may also evidence the proficiency of the internal audit activity, individual internal auditors, or both.

Any of the following documents could evidence the conformance of the internal audit activity as a whole:

- The internal audit plan that includes an analysis of resource requirements.
- An inventory of available audit staff skills or individual profiles listing qualifications.
- An assurance map with a list of qualifications of service providers on which the internal audit activity relies.
- Documented results of internal assessments.

IG1220 – Due Professional Care

> ### Standard 1220 – Due Professional Care
>
> Internal auditors must apply the care and skill expected of a reasonably prudent and competent internal auditor. Due professional care does not imply infallibility.

Getting Started

Obtaining appropriate education, experience, certifications, and training helps internal auditors develop the level of skill and expertise required to perform their duties with due professional care. Additionally, internal auditors should understand and apply the Mandatory Guidance of the International Professional Practices Framework (IPPF) and may find it helpful to become familiar with the core competencies described in The IIA's Global Internal Audit Competency Framework.

At the engagement level, applying due professional care involves comprehending the objectives and scope of the engagement, as well as the competencies that will be required to execute the audit work and any policies and procedures specific to the internal audit activity and the organization.

Considerations for Implementation

For internal auditors, due professional care requires conformance with The IIA's Code of Ethics and may entail conformance with the organization's code of conduct and any additional codes of conduct relevant to other professional designations attained. The internal audit activity may have a formal process that requires internal auditors to sign an annual declaration related to The IIA's Code of Ethics or the organization's code of conduct.

Along with the IPPF, the internal audit activity's policies and procedures provide a systematic and disciplined approach to planning, executing, and documenting internal audit work. By following this systematic and disciplined approach, internal auditors essentially apply due professional care. However, what constitutes due professional care partially depends upon the complexities of the engagement. Standards 1220.A1, 1220.A2, 1220.A3, and 1220.C1 describe the elements that internal auditors must consider in exercising due professional care. For example, internal auditors must consider the possibility of significant errors, fraud, and noncompliance and are expected to conduct examinations and verifications to the same extent as would a reasonably prudent and competent internal auditor in the same or similar circumstances. Yet, Standard 1220 also specifies that due professional care does not imply infallibility. Therefore, internal auditors are not expected to give absolute assurance that noncompliance or irregularities do not exist.

To ensure due professional care at the engagement level, Standard 2340—Engagement Supervision requires engagements to be properly supervised, which generally involves supervisory review of the engagement workpapers, results, and conclusions to be reported. After such reviews, supervisors usually provide feedback to the internal auditors who conducted the engagement, often through post-engagement meetings. Input about internal auditors' due professional care may be solicited through post-engagement surveys of audit clients.

In managing the internal audit activity (2000 series of standards) and implementing a quality assurance and improvement program (1300 series of standards), the chief audit executive (CAE) assumes overall responsibility for ensuring that due professional care is applied. Thus, the CAE typically develops measurement tools such as self-assessments, metrics such as key performance indicators, and a process to assess the performance of individual internal auditors and the internal audit activity as a whole. In addition to client surveys, tools to evaluate individual internal auditors could include peer and supervisory reviews. The internal audit activity as a whole may be evaluated through internal and external assessments, in accordance with standards 1310 through 1312, as well as client surveys or similar methods of feedback.

Considerations for Demonstrating Conformance

Internal auditors demonstrate conformance with Standard 1220 through proper application of the IPPF's Mandatory Guidance, which would be reflected in their engagement plans, work programs, and workpapers. Performance reviews of internal auditors may reference their application of due professional care. Appropriate supervisory reviews of engagements is likely to be documented in workpapers. Due professional care may also be evidenced when the engagement supervisor conducts post-engagement staff meetings and solicits feedback from audit clients through surveys or other tools. Additionally, evidence may include an annual declaration related to The IIA's Code of Ethics and organization's code of conduct. Finally, internal and external assessments performed as part of the internal audit activity's quality assurance and improvement program also may indicate that due professional care has been maintained.

| Mission | Core Principles | Definition | Standards |

▶ Standard 1230 – Continuing Professional Development

Internal auditors must enhance their knowledge, skills, and other competencies through continuing professional development.

▶ IG1230 – Continuing Professional Development

Getting Started

In order to enhance their competencies and continue their professional development, internal auditors may want to reflect on their job requirements, including the training policies and the professional education requirements of their profession, organization, industry, and any certifications or areas of specialization. Additionally, internal auditors may consider feedback from recent performance reviews, assessment results regarding their conformance with the Mandatory Guidance of the International Professional Practices Framework (IPPF), and the results of self-assessments based on The IIA's Global Internal Audit Competency Framework, or a similar benchmark. Reflecting on career goals may help internal auditors with long-term planning of their professional development.

Considerations for Implementation

An individual internal auditor may use a self-assessment tool, such as the Competency Framework, as a basis for creating a professional development plan. The development plan may encompass on-the-job training, coaching, mentoring, and other internal and external training, volunteer, or certification opportunities. Typically, the internal auditor discusses the plan with the chief audit executive (CAE), and the two may agree to use the professional development plan as the basis for developing measures of the internal auditor's performance (i.e., key performance indicators), which could be incorporated into supervisory reviews, client surveys, and annual performance reviews. The results of the reviews can help the CAE and the internal auditor prioritize areas for continuing professional development. Ultimately, the individual internal auditor is responsible for conforming with Standard 1230.

Opportunities for professional development include participating in conferences, seminars, training programs, online courses and webinars, self-study programs, or classroom courses; conducting research projects; volunteering with professional organizations; and pursuing professional certifications such as The IIA's Certified Internal Auditor® (CIA®). Continuing professional development related to a certain industry or specialization (e.g., data analytics, financial services, IT, taxation law, or systems design) may lead to additional professional competencies that could enhance internal audit work in those specific areas.

At times, internal audit client surveys may reveal a concern regarding internal auditors' business acumen. The CAE and internal auditors can address such concerns by participating on various training or opportunities offered within their organization to better understand the business.

To ensure internal auditors have the opportunity to enhance their knowledge, skills, and other competencies, the CAE may establish a training and development policy that supports continuing professional development. Such a policy may specify a minimum number of training hours for each auditor, such as 40 hours, which is consistent with many professional certification requirements. CAEs may consider using benchmarking to assess current and emerging needs of the internal profession, as well as specific trends within the industry or specialized area.

To ensure their internal audit knowledge stays current on a day-to-day basis, internal auditors may seek guidance from The IIA regarding standards, best practices, procedures, and techniques that could affect the internal audit profession or their organization and specific industry. This may involve maintaining current memberships in The IIA and other professional organizations, networking at local events, and monitoring or subscribing to feeds or notification services related to the internal audit profession and industry-specific news.

Considerations for Demonstrating Conformance

Internal auditors may demonstrate conformance with Standard 1230 by retaining documentation or other evidence of any of the following:

- Self-assessments against a competency framework or benchmark.
- Professional development and training plans.

- Memberships and participation in professional organizations.
- Subscriptions to sources of professional information.
- Completed training (e.g., continuing education credits, certifications, or certificates of completion).

Enhanced proficiency achieved through on-the-job training and in-house training is likely to be noted in performance evaluations, which may also track opportunities for future professional development. Performance metrics may reflect supervisory or peer observations of new skills and enhanced capabilities. Internal audit policies, a training schedule, and internal audit staff surveys may evidence that opportunities for the continuing professional development were provided by the CAE.

IG1300 – Quality Assurance and Improvement Program

Getting Started

Standard 1300 tasks the chief audit executive (CAE) with developing and maintaining a comprehensive quality assurance and improvement program (QAIP). The QAIP should encompass all aspects of operating and managing the internal audit activity—including consulting engagements—as found in the mandatory elements of the International Professional Practices Framework (IPPF). It may also be beneficial for the QAIP to consider best practices in the internal audit profession.

The QAIP is designed to enable an evaluation of the internal audit activity's conformance with the *International Standards for the Professional Practice of Internal Auditing* (*Standards*) and whether internal auditors apply The IIA's Code of Ethics. As such, it must include ongoing and periodic internal assessments as well as external assessments by a qualified independent assessor or assessment team (see Standard 1310—Requirements of the Quality Assurance and Improvement Program).

The CAE must have a thorough understanding of the mandatory elements of the IPPF, especially the *Standards* and the Code of Ethics. Generally, the CAE meets with the board to gain an understanding of the expectations for the internal audit activity, to discuss the importance of the *Standards* and the QAIP, and to encourage the board's support of these.

Typically, the CAE finds examples of how QAIPs are developed and implemented in other organizations—particularly those that are similar in nature and maturity—for benchmarking purposes. Additionally, the CAE may wish to consult IIA Supplemental Guidance and other published guidance on the matter, including The IIA's *Quality Assessment Manual for the Internal Audit Activity*.

▶ Standard 1300 – Quality Assurance and Improvement Program

The chief audit executive must develop and maintain a quality assurance and improvement program that covers all aspects of the internal audit activity.

Interpretation:

A quality assurance and improvement program is designed to enable an evaluation of the internal audit activity's conformance with the Standards *and an evaluation of whether internal auditors apply the Code of Ethics. The program also assesses the efficiency and effectiveness of the internal audit activity and identifies opportunities for improvement. The chief audit executive should encourage board oversight in the quality assurance and improvement program.*

Considerations for Implementation

A well-developed QAIP ensures that the concept of quality is embedded in the internal audit activity and all of its operations. The internal audit activity should not need to assess whether each individual engagement conforms with the *Standards*. Rather, engagements should be undertaken in accordance with an established methodology that promotes quality and, by default, conformance with the *Standards*. Additionally, the methodology generally promotes continuous improvement of the internal audit activity.

As Standard 1300 requires, the CAE develops and maintains a QAIP that covers all aspects of the internal audit activity, with the ultimate goal of developing an internal audit activity with a scope and quality of work that includes conformance with the *Standards* and whether internal auditors apply the Code of Ethics. The QAIP enables an internal audit activity to be evaluated for conformance with the *Standards* and whether internal auditors apply and the Code of Ethics. As such, the QAIP includes assessments of the internal audit activity's efficiency and effectiveness, which help to identify opportunities for improvement.

The CAE periodically evaluates the QAIP and updates it as needed. For example, as the internal audit activity matures, or as conditions within the internal audit activity change, adjustments to the QAIP may become necessary to ensure that it continues to operate in an effective and efficient manner and to assure stakeholders that it adds value by improving the organization's operations.

To implement Standard 1300, the CAE must consider the requirements related to its five essential components:

- Internal assessments (Standard 1311).
- External assessments (Standard 1312).
- Communication of QAIP results (Standard 1320).
- Proper use of a conformance statement (Standard 1321).
- Disclosure of nonconformance (Standard 1322).

Internal Assessments

Internal assessments consist of ongoing monitoring and periodic self-assessments (see Standard 1311—Internal Assessments), which evaluate the internal audit activity's conformance with the mandatory elements of the IPPF, the quality and supervision of audit work performed, the adequacy of internal audit policies and procedures, the value the internal audit activity adds to the organization, and the establishment and achievement of key performance indicators.

The CAE should establish ongoing monitoring and ensure that reviews of the internal audit activity occur periodically. Ongoing monitoring is achieved primarily through continuous activities such as engagement planning and supervision, standardized work practices, workpaper procedures and signoffs, report reviews, as well as identification of any weaknesses or areas in need of improvement and action plans to address them. Ongoing monitoring helps the CAE determine whether internal audit processes are delivering quality on an engagement-by-engagement basis.

Periodic self-assessments are conducted to validate that ongoing monitoring is operating effectively and to assess whether the internal audit activity is in conformance with the *Standards* and whether internal auditors apply the Code of Ethics. Through conformance with the *Standards* and the Code of Ethics, the internal audit activity also achieves alignment with the Definition of Internal Auditing and the Core Principles for the Professional Practice of Internal Auditing.

Implementation Guide 1311—Internal Assessments provides further guidance on the QAIP requirement for internal assessments.

External Assessments

In addition to internal assessments, the CAE is responsible for ensuring that the internal audit activity conducts an external assessment at least once every five years (see Standard 1312—External Assessments). The purpose of the assessment, which must be performed by an independent assessor or assessment team from outside the organization, is to validate whether the internal audit activity conforms with the *Standards* and whether internal auditors apply the Code of Ethics.

A self-assessment may be performed in lieu of a full external assessment, provided it is validated by a qualified, independent, competent, and professional external assessor. In such cases, the scope of the self-assessment with external independent validation would consist of a comprehensive and fully documented self-assessment process that emulates the full external process, and an independent, onsite validation by a qualified, independent assessor.

Implementation Guides 1312—External Assessments provides further guidance on the QAIP requirement for external assessments.

Communication of QAIP Results

The CAE must communicate the results of the QAIP to senior management and the board, as stated in Standard 1320—Reporting on the Quality Assurance and Improvement Program. Such communication should include:

- The scope and frequency of both internal and external assessments.
- The qualifications and independence of the assessor(s) or assessment team.
- The conclusions of the assessors.
- Any corrective action plans that have been created from the assessments to address areas that were not in conformance with the *Standards*, along with opportunities for improvement.

Implementation Guide 1320—Reporting on the Quality Assurance and Improvement Program provides further guidance on QAIP reporting.

Proper Use of a Conformance Statement

The internal audit activity may only communicate—in writing or verbally—that the internal audit activity conforms with the *Standards* if results of both the QAIP's internal and external assessments support such a statement. Implementation Guide 1321—Use of "Conforms with the *International Standards for the Professional Practice of Internal Auditing*" provides further guidance on the proper use of a conformance statement.

Disclosure of Nonconformance

If an internal or external assessment concludes that the internal audit activity does not conform with the IPPF's mandatory elements, and the lack of conformance impacts the overall scope or operation of the internal audit activity, the CAE must disclose the nonconformance and its impact to senior management and the board. Implementation Guide 1322—Disclosure of Nonconformance provides further guidance on how and when to report nonconformance.

Considerations for Demonstrating Conformance

Multiple activities and documents may demonstrate conformance with Standard 1300, the most notable of which are the CAE's documented QAIP itself, the results of internal and external assessments, and documentation showing the CAE's communication of QAIP results with the board. The latter typically consists of findings, corrective action plans, and corrective actions taken to improve the internal audit activity's conformance with the *Standards* and the Code of Ethics. Additionally, any documentation of actions taken to improve the internal audit activity's efficiency and effectiveness may help demonstrate conformance with the standard. For external assessments, documentation from the external assessor or assessment team, or written independent validation of a self-assessment, may be used to indicate conformance with Standard 1300. Board meeting minutes where QAIPs and their results were discussed and presentations to the board or senior management may also help evidence conformance.

Mission | Core Principles | Definition | Standards

> **Standard 1310 – Requirements of the Quality Assurance and Improvement Program**
>
> The quality assurance and improvement program must include both internal and external assessments.

▶ IG1310 – Requirements of the Quality Assurance and Improvement Program

Getting Started

Standard 1310 communicates the requirements that make up the quality assurance and improvement program (QAIP), which covers all aspects of the internal audit activity. Specifically, the standard indicates that both internal and external assessments are required.

The chief audit executive (CAE) should be aware of these requirements. Internal assessments are composed of rigorous, comprehensive processes, continuous supervision and testing of internal audit and consulting work, and periodic validations of conformance with the *International Standards for the Professional Practice of Internal Auditing* (*Standards*) and whether internal auditors apply the Code of Ethics. External assessments provide an opportunity for an independent assessor or assessment team to conclude as to the internal audit activity's conformance with the *Standards* and whether internal auditors apply the Code of Ethics, and to identify areas for improvement. The QAIP also includes ongoing measurements and analyses of performance metrics such as accomplishment of the internal audit plan, cycle time, recommendations accepted, and customer satisfaction.

Typically, the CAE would be aware of any prior results from both internal and external assessments that indicate areas upon which the internal audit activity can improve. The CAE would implement action plans related to any identified improvements through the QAIP.

Considerations for Implementation

Standard 1310 requires the QAIP to include both internal and external assessments. Internal assessments consist of ongoing monitoring and periodic self-assessments (see Standard 1311—Internal Assessments), which evaluate the internal audit activity's conformance with the mandatory elements of the IPPF, the quality and supervision of audit work performed, the adequacy of internal audit policies and procedures, the value the internal audit activity adds to the organization, and the establishment and achievement of key performance indicators.

The CAE should establish ongoing monitoring and ensure that reviews of the internal audit activity occur periodically. Ongoing monitoring is achieved primarily through continuous activities such as engagement planning and supervision, standardized work practices, workpaper procedures and signoffs, report reviews, as well as identification of any weaknesses or areas in need of improvement and action plans to address them. Continuous monitoring helps the CAE determine whether internal audit processes are delivering quality on an engagement-by-engagement basis.

Periodic self-assessments are conducted to validate that ongoing monitoring is operating effectively and to assess whether the internal audit activity is in conformance with the *Standards* and whether internal auditors apply the Code of Ethics. Through conformance with the *Standards* and the Code of Ethics, the internal audit activity also achieves alignment with the Definition of Internal Auditing and the Core Principles for the Professional Practice of Internal Auditing.

In addition to internal assessments, the CAE is responsible for ensuring that the internal audit activity conducts an external assessment at least once every five years (see Standard 1312—External Assessments). The purpose of the assessment, which must be performed by an independent assessor or assessment team from outside the organization, is to validate whether the internal audit activity conforms with the *Standards* and whether internal auditors apply the Code of Ethics.

A self-assessment may be performed in lieu of a full external assessment, provided it is validated by a qualified, independent, competent, and professional external assessor. In such cases, the scope of the self-assessment with external independent validation would consist of a comprehensive and fully documented self-assessment process that emulates the full external process, and an independent, onsite validation by a qualified, independent external assessor.

The implementation guides for Standard 1311 and Standard 1312 provide further guidance on the QAIP requirements for internal and external assessments.

Considerations for Demonstrating Conformance

Multiple items may indicate conformance with Standard 1310, including all documentation that demonstrates conformance with Standard 1311 and Standard 1312. Additionally, conformance may be demonstrated by minutes of board meetings where plans for—and results of—assessments were discussed. A benchmarking report and requests for services may show the organization's due diligence in vetting external assessors.

Specific to internal assessments, any evidence that ongoing monitoring activities were completed according to the internal audit activity's QAIP may demonstrate conformance (e.g., key performance indicator reviews or workpaper reviews). In addition, conformance may be demonstrated by documentation of periodic assessments that have been completed, including the scope of review and approach plan, workpapers, and communication reports. Finally, QAIP results (e.g., corrective action plans, corrective actions taken to improve conformance, actions taken to improve efficiency and effectiveness) may indicate conformance.

For external assessments, the most important indicator of conformance is the external assessor's report, which includes a conclusion as to the degree of conformance and corrective action plans. This report often includes recommendations from the external assessor on ways to improve internal audit quality, efficiency, and effectiveness, which may help the internal audit activity better serve the organization's stakeholders and add value.

▶ IG1311 – Internal Assessments

Getting Started

As Standard 1311 indicates, the chief audit executive (CAE) is responsible for ensuring that the internal audit activity conducts an internal assessment that includes both ongoing monitoring and periodic self-assessments. Internal assessments validate that the internal audit activity continues to conform with the *International Standards for the Professional Practice of Internal Auditing* (*Standards*) and the Code of Ethics. The CAE understands that the internal assessments focus on continuous improvement of the internal audit activity and involves monitoring its efficiency and effectiveness.

The IIA's *Quality Assessment Manual for the Internal Audit Activity* or comparable guidance and tools may serve as a guide to conducting an internal assessment.

Considerations for Implementation

The two interrelated parts of internal assessments—ongoing monitoring and periodic self-assessments—provide an effective structure for the internal audit activity to continuously assess its conformance with the *Standards* and whether internal auditors apply the Code of Ethics. Additionally, they may allow for identification of improvement opportunities.

Ongoing Monitoring

Ongoing monitoring is achieved primarily through continuous activities such as engagement planning and supervision, standardized work practices, workpaper procedures and signoffs, report reviews, as well as identification of any weaknesses or areas in need of improvement and action plans to address them. Ongoing monitoring helps the CAE determine whether internal audit processes are delivering quality on an engagement-by-engagement basis. Generally, ongoing monitoring occurs routinely throughout the year via the implementation of standard work practices. To facilitate this, the CAE may develop templates for

---

▶ Standard 1311 – Internal Assessments

Internal assessments must include:

- Ongoing monitoring of the performance of the internal audit activity.
- Periodic self-assessments or assessments by other persons within the organization with sufficient knowledge of internal audit practices.

Interpretation:

Ongoing monitoring is an integral part of the day-to-day supervision, review, and measurement of the internal audit activity. Ongoing monitoring is incorporated into the routine policies and practices used to manage the internal audit activity and uses processes, tools, and information considered necessary to evaluate conformance with the Code of Ethics and the Standards.

Periodic assessments are conducted to evaluate conformance with the Code of Ethics and the Standards.

Sufficient knowledge of internal audit practices requires at least an understanding of all elements of the International Professional Practices Framework.

| Mission | Core Principles | Definition | Standards |

internal auditors to use throughout engagements, ensuring consistency in the application of the *Standards*.

Adequate supervision is a fundamental element of any quality assurance and improvement program (QAIP). Supervision begins with planning and continues throughout the performance and communication phases of the engagement. Adequate supervision is ensured through expectation-setting, ongoing communications among internal auditors throughout the engagement, and workpaper review procedures, including timely sign-off by the individual responsible for supervising engagements. Implementation Guide 2340 – Engagement Supervision provides further guidance on internal audit supervision.

The implementation guides for the following series of standards provide further guidance on appropriate performance of an engagement, from engagement planning through the dissemination of results: 2200, 2300, and 2400.

Additional mechanisms commonly used for ongoing monitoring include:

- Checklists or automation tools to provide assurance on internal auditors' compliance with established practices and procedures and to ensure consistency in the application of performance standards.

- Feedback from internal audit clients and other stakeholders regarding the efficiency and effectiveness of the internal audit team. Feedback may be solicited immediately following the engagement or on a periodic basis (e.g., semi-annually or annually) via survey tools or conversations between the CAE and management.

- Staff and engagement key performance indicators (KPIs), such as the number of certified internal auditors on staff, their years of experience in internal auditing, the number of continuing professional development hours they earned during the year, timeliness of engagements, and stakeholder satisfaction.

- Other measurements that may be valuable in determining the efficiency and effectiveness of the internal audit activity. Measures of project budgets, timekeeping systems, and audit plan completion may help to determine whether the appropriate amount of time is spent on all aspects of the audit engagement. Budget-to-actual variance can also be valuable measurement to determine the efficiency and effectiveness of the internal audit activity.

In addition to validating conformance with the *Standards* and the Code of Ethics, ongoing monitoring may identify opportunities to improve the internal audit activity. In such cases, the CAE typically addresses these opportunities and may develop an action plan. Once changes are implemented, key performance indicators can be used to monitor success. Results of ongoing monitoring should be reported to the board at least annually, as required by Standard 1320—Reporting on the Quality Assurance and Improvement Program.

Periodic Self-assessments

Periodic self-assessments have a different focus than ongoing monitoring in that they generally provide a more holistic, comprehensive review of the *Standards* and the internal audit activity. In contrast, ongoing monitoring is generally focused on reviews conducted at the engagement level. Additionally, periodic self-assessments address conformance with every standard, whereas ongoing monitoring frequently is more focused on the performance standards at the engagement level.

Periodic self-assessments are generally conducted by senior members of the internal audit activity, a dedicated quality assurance team or individual within the internal audit activity who has extensive experience with the International Professional Practices Framework (IPPF), Certified Internal Auditors, or other competent internal audit professionals who may be assigned elsewhere in the organization. Whenever possible, it is advantageous to include internal audit activity staff in the self-assessment process, as it can serve as a useful training opportunity to improve internal auditors' understanding of the IPPF.

The internal audit activity conducts periodic self-assessments to validate its continued conformance with the *Standards* and the Code of Ethics and to evaluate:

- The quality and supervision of work performed.
- The adequacy and appropriateness of internal audit policies and procedures.
- The ways in which the internal audit activity adds value.
- The achievement of key performance indicators.
- The degree to which stakeholder expectations are met.

To accomplish this, the individual or team conducting the self-assessment typically assesses each standard to determine whether the internal audit activity is operating in conformance. This may include in-depth interviews and surveys of stakeholders. Through this process, the CAE is typically able to assess the quality of the internal audit activity's audit practices, including adherence to policies and procedures for conducting engagements. Periodic self-assessments may be conducted by a member of the internal audit activity or by other persons within the organization with sufficient knowledge of internal audit practices, specifically the *Standards* and the Code of Ethics.

The internal audit activity may perform additional steps to support the periodic self-assessment, such as conducting post-engagement reviews or analyzing key performance indicators (KPIs).

- **Post-engagement review**—The internal audit activity may select a sample of engagements from a particular timeframe and conduct a review to assess compliance with internal audit policies (see Standard 2040—Policies and Procedures) and conformance with the *Standards* and the Code of Ethics. These reviews are typically conducted by internal audit staff who were not involved in the respective engagement. In a larger or more mature organization, this process may be handled by a quality assurance specialist or team. In smaller organizations, the CAE or the individual responsible for reviewing workpapers may use a checklist, completed after the final report is issued, to accomplish this review and close the file.

- **KPI analysis**—The internal audit activity may also monitor and analyze KPIs related to the efficiency of standard internal audit work practices (e.g., budget-to-actual engagement hours, percentage of the audit plan completed, number of days between fieldwork completion and report issuance, percentage of audit observations implemented, and timeliness of corrections related to audit observations). Other commonly used metrics include the number of certified internal auditors on staff, their years of experience in internal auditing, and the number of continuing professional development hours they earned during the year.

Following a periodic self-assessment, where appropriate, the CAE may develop an action plan to address opportunities for improvement. This plan should include proposed timelines for actions.

Results of periodic self-assessments, which indicate the internal audit activity's level of conformance with the *Standards* and the Code of Ethics, must be communicated to the board upon completion, as required by Standard 1320. A periodic self-assessment performed shortly before an external assessment may help reduce the time and effort required to complete the external assessment (see Standard 1312—External Assessments).

Considerations for Demonstrating Conformance

Multiple items may indicate conformance with Standard 1311, including any evidence that ongoing monitoring activities were completed according to the internal audit activity's QAIP. Examples may include completed checklists that support workpaper reviews, survey results, and KPIs related to the efficiency and effectiveness of the internal audit activity, such as an analysis of budget-to-actual engagement hours. In addition, conformance may be demonstrated by documentation of completed periodic assessments, which include the scope of the review and approach plan, workpapers, and communication reports. Finally, presentations to the board and management, meeting minutes, and the results of both ongoing monitoring and periodic self-assessment—including corrective action plans and corrective actions taken to improve conformance, efficiency, and effectiveness—may indicate conformance.

| Mission | Core Principles | Definition | Standards |

> # Standard 1312 – External Assessments

External assessments must be conducted at least once every five years by a qualified, independent assessor or assessment team from outside the organization. The chief audit executive must discuss with the board:

- The form and frequency of external assessment.
- The qualifications and independence of the external assessor or assessment team, including any potential conflict of interest.

Interpretation:

External assessments may be accomplished through a full external assessment, or a self-assessment with independent external validation. The external assessor must conclude as to conformance with the Code of Ethics and the Standards*; the external assessment may also include operational or strategic comments.*

A qualified assessor or assessment team demonstrates competence in two areas: the professional practice of internal auditing and the external

(Continued on next page)

> ## IG1312 – External Assessments

Getting Started

As this standard indicates, the chief audit executive (CAE) is responsible for ensuring that the internal audit activity conducts an external assessment at least once every five years by an independent assessor or assessment team from outside the organization. A requirement of the internal audit activity's quality and assurance improvement program (QAIP), the external assessment validates that the internal audit activity conforms with the *International Standards for the Professional Practice of Internal Auditing* (*Standards*) and internal auditors apply the Code of Ethics. Thus, it is crucial that the CAE regularly reviews the International Professional Practices Framework (IPPF) and is aware of any changes that may need to be communicated throughout the internal audit activity.

The CAE typically has an understanding of different types of external assessments as well as various resources available to provide such services. The CAE is also typically aware of any procurement policies his or her organization may have related to securing an external services provider. In addition, the CAE should be aware of independence requirements for the external assessor or assessment team and understand situations that may impair independence or objectivity, or create a conflict of interest.

Considerations for Implementation

Typically, the CAE has discussions with senior management and the board regarding the frequency and type of external assessment that will be performed. Such discussions enable the CAE to educate stakeholders and to gain an understanding of, and appreciation for, the organization's expectations.

The *Standards* require the internal audit activity to undergo an external assessment at least once every five years. However, upon discussing these requirements with senior management and the board, the CAE may determine that it is appropriate to conduct an external assessment more frequently. There are several reasons to consider a more frequent review, including changes in leadership (e.g., senior management or the CAE), significant changes in internal audit policies or procedures, the merger of two or more audit organizations into one internal audit activity, or significant staff turnover. Additionally, industry-specific or environmental issues may warrant more frequent review.

External assessments assess the internal audit activity's conformance with the *Standards* and provide an evaluation of whether the internal auditors apply the Code of Ethics. As noted in Standard 1320—Reporting on the Quality Assurance and Improvement Program, the external assessment results, including the assessor's or the assessment team's conclusion on conformance, must be communicated to senior management and the board upon completion.

Two Approaches

External assessments may be accomplished using one of two approaches: a full external assessment, or a self-assessment with independent external validation (SAIV). A full external assessment would be conducted by a qualified, independent external assessor or assessment team. The team should be comprised of competent professionals and led by an experienced and professional project team leader. The scope of a full external assessment typically includes three core components:

- The level of conformance with the *Standards* and the Code of Ethics. This may be evaluated via a review of the internal audit activity's charter, plans, policies, procedures, and practices. In some cases, the review may also include applicable legislative and regulatory requirements.

- The efficiency and effectiveness of the internal audit activity. This may be measured through an assessment of the internal audit activity's processes and infrastructure, including the QAIP, and an evaluation of the internal audit staff's knowledge, experience, and expertise.

- The extent to which the internal audit activity meets expectations of the board, senior management, and operations management, and adds value to the organization.

> (Continued)
>
> *assessment process. Competence can be demonstrated through a mixture of experience and theoretical learning. Experience gained in organizations of similar size, complexity, sector or industry, and technical issues is more valuable than less relevant experience. In the case of an assessment team, not all members of the team need to have all the competencies; it is the team as a whole that is qualified. The chief audit executive uses professional judgment when assessing whether an assessor or assessment team demonstrates sufficient competence to be qualified.*
>
> *An independent assessor or assessment team means not having either an actual or a perceived conflict of interest and not being a part of, or under the control of, the organization to which the internal audit activity belongs. The chief audit executive should encourage board oversight in the external assessment to reduce perceived or potential conflicts of interest.*

The second approach to meeting the requirement for an external assessment is an SAIV. This type of external assessment typically is conducted by the internal audit activity and then validated by a qualified, independent external assessor. The scope of an SAIV typically consists of:

- A comprehensive and fully documented self-assessment process that emulates the full external assessment process, at least with respect to evaluating the internal audit activity's conformance with the *Standards* and the Code of Ethics.
- Onsite validation by a qualified, independent external assessor.
- Limited attention to other areas such as benchmarking; review, consultation, and employment of leading practices; and interviews with senior and operations management.

External Assessor Qualifications

Regardless of which approach is selected for the external assessment, a qualified, independent external assessor or assessment team must be retained to complete the assessment. The CAE usually consults with senior management and the board to select the assessor or assessment team. Assessors or assessment teams must be competent in two main areas: the professional practice of internal auditing (including current in-depth knowledge of the IPPF), and the external quality assessment process. Preferred qualifications and competencies generally include:

- Certification as an internal audit professional (e.g., Certified Internal Auditor).
- Knowledge of leading internal auditing practices.
- Sufficient recent experience in the practice of internal auditing at a management level, which demonstrates a working knowledge and application of the IPPF.

Organizations may seek additional qualifications and competencies for assessment team leaders and independent validators, including:

- An additional level of competence and experience gained from previous external assessment work.

- Completion of The IIA's quality assessment training course or similar training.
- CAE (or comparable senior internal audit management) experience.
- Relevant technical expertise and industry experience.

Individuals with expertise in other areas may provide assistance, as appropriate. Examples include specialists in enterprise risk management, IT auditing, statistical sampling, monitoring systems, and control self-assessment.

The CAE should determine the skills desired for the external assessment and use professional judgment to select the assessor or assessment team. Based on the needs of the internal audit activity, for example, the CAE may prefer individuals with internal audit experience in an organization of a similar size, complexity, and industry, as these professionals may be more valuable. Each individual on the team does not need to possess all of the preferred competencies; rather, the team as a whole should possess the necessary qualifications to provide the best results.

Assessor Independence and Objectivity

The CAE, senior management, and the board should consider and discuss several factors related to independence and objectivity when selecting an external assessor or assessment team. External assessors, assessment teams, and their organizations should be free from actual, potential, or perceived conflicts of interest that could impair objectivity. Potential impairments may include past, present, or future relationships with the organization, its personnel, or its internal audit activity (e.g., external audit of financial statements; assistance to the internal audit activity; personal relationships; previous or future participation in internal quality assessments; or consulting services in governance, risk management, financial reporting, internal control, or other related areas).

In cases where the potential assessors are former employees of the internal audit activity's organization, consideration should be given to the length of time the assessor has been independent. (Independent, in this context, means not having a conflict of interest and not being a part of, or under the influence of, the organization to which the internal audit activity belongs).

Individuals from another department of the organization, although organizationally separate from the internal audit activity, are not considered independent for the purpose of conducting an external assessment. In the public sector, internal audit activities in separate entities within the same tier of government are not considered independent if they report to the same CAE. Likewise, individuals from a related organization (e.g., a parent organization; an affiliate in the same group of entities; or an entity with regular oversight, supervision, or quality assurance responsibilities with respect to the subject organization) are not considered independent.

Reciprocal peer assessments between two organizations would not be considered independent. However, reciprocal assessments among three or more peer organizations—organizations within the same industry, regional association, or other affinity group—may be considered independent. Still, care must be exercised to ensure that independence and objectivity are not impaired and all team members are able to exercise their responsibilities fully.

Considerations for Demonstrating Conformance

The external assessor's report is the primary document used to demonstrate conformance with Standard 1312. This report often includes recommendations from the external assessor and management action plans to improve internal audit quality, efficiency, and effectiveness, which may provide new ideas or ways for the internal audit activity to better serve the organization's stakeholders and add value.

Additional documents that may help demonstrate conformance include minutes of board meetings where plans for, and results of, external assessments were discussed. A benchmarking report and requests for services may show the organization's due diligence in vetting external assessors.

IG1320 – Reporting on the Quality Assurance and Improvement Program

Getting Started

Standard 1320 communicates the minimum criteria that the chief audit executive (CAE) must communicate to senior management and the board related to the quality assurance and improvement program (QAIP). Reviewing the requirements related to each element in the standard may help the CAE prepare to implement this standard.

As this standard indicates, the CAE is responsible for communicating results of the entire program. To do this, the CAE must understand the requirements of the QAIP (see Standard 1300—Quality Assurance and Improvement Program). Typically, the CAE meets regularly with senior management and the board to understand and agree upon the expectations for communications surrounding the internal audit activity, including those regarding the QAIP. The CAE also considers the responsibilities related to the QAIP that are outlined in the internal audit charter.

The CAE should be aware of any internal assessments, including periodic assessments and ongoing monitoring, as well as completed external assessments. As such, the CAE should have an understanding of the internal audit activity's degree of conformance with the *International Standards for the Professional Practice of Internal Auditing* (*Standards*) and The IIA's Code of Ethics.

Considerations for Implementation

Typically, details regarding the QAIP are documented in the policies and procedures manual for the internal audit activity (see Standard 2040—Policies and Procedures) and the internal audit charter (see Standard 1010—Recognizing Mandatory Guidance in the Internal Audit Charter). The CAE may begin by reviewing this information to understand the communication requirements related to reporting on the QAIP, which include four core elements:

Standard 1320 – Reporting on the Quality Assurance and Improvement Program

The chief audit executive must communicate the results of the quality assurance and improvement program to senior management and the board. Disclosure should include:

- The scope and frequency of both the internal and external assessments.
- The qualifications and independence of the assessor(s) or assessment team, including potential conflicts of interest.
- Conclusions of assessors.
- Corrective action plans.

Interpretation:

The form, content, and frequency of communicating the results of the quality assurance and improvement program is established through discussions with senior management and the board and considers the responsibilities of the internal audit activity and chief audit executive as contained in the internal audit

(Continued on next page)

> (Continued)
>
> *charter. To demonstrate conformance with the Code of Ethics and the* Standards, *the results of external and periodic internal assessments are communicated upon completion of such assessments, and the results of ongoing monitoring are communicated at least annually. The results include the assessor's or assessment team's evaluation with respect to the degree of conformance.*

- Scope and frequency of internal and external assessments.
- Qualifications and independence of the assessors.
- Conclusions of assessors.
- Corrective action plans.

Scope and Frequency of Internal and External Assessments

The scope and frequency of both internal and external assessments must be discussed with the board and senior management (see Standard 1311—Internal Assessments and Standard 1312—External Assessments). The scope should consider the responsibilities of the internal audit activity and the CAE, as contained in the internal audit charter. The scope may include board and senior management expectations of the internal audit activity, as well as expectations expressed by other stakeholders. It may also include internal audit practices assessed against the *Standards,* as well as any other regulatory requirements that may impact the internal audit activity. The frequency of external assessments varies depending on the size and maturity of the internal audit activity.

Internal Assessments

The CAE must establish a means for communicating the results of internal assessments at least annually to enhance the credibility and objectivity of the internal audit activity. The Interpretation of Standard 1320 states that the results of periodic internal assessment should be communicated upon completion of such assessments, and the results of ongoing monitoring should be completed at least annually.

Periodic internal assessments may include an evaluation of the internal audit activity's conformance with the *Standards* to support the internal audit activity's statement of conformance (see Standard 1321—Use of "Conforms with the *International Standards for the Professional Practice of Internal Auditing*"). Larger organizations may conduct periodic internal assessments annually, while smaller or less mature internal audit activities, may perform them less frequently (e.g., every two years). For example, the internal audit activity may perform a periodic assessment over a multi-year period, and report on the results of the work conducted during each period separately.

Ongoing monitoring typically includes reporting on internal audit key performance indicators. The CAE may provide an annual report to senior management and the board regarding the results of ongoing monitoring and include any recommendations for improvement.

Generally, those assigned responsibility for conducting ongoing monitoring and periodic internal assessments communicate the results directly to the CAE while performing the assessments. In a smaller internal audit activity, the CAE may take a greater direct role in the internal assessment process. The results of internal assessments include, where appropriate, corrective action plans and progress against completion. The CAE may distribute internal assessment reports to various stakeholders, including senior management, the board, and external auditors.

Implementation Guide 1311—Internal Assessments provides additional detail regarding ongoing monitoring and periodic internal assessments.

External assessments

The CAE must discuss the frequency of external assessments with senior management and the board. The *Standards* require the internal audit activity to undergo an external assessment at least once every five years. However, upon discussing these requirements with the senior management and the board, the CAE may determine that it is appropriate to conduct an external assessment more frequently. There are several reasons to consider a more frequent review, including changes in leadership (e.g., senior management or the CAE), significant changes in internal audit policies or procedures, the merger of two or more audit organizations into one internal audit activity, or significant staff turnover. Additionally, industry-specific or environmental issues may warrant more frequent review.

Qualifications and Independence of the Assessors

When selecting an external assessor or assessment team, the CAE typically discusses with senior management and the board the qualifications of the potential assessor(s) and several factors related to independence and objectivity, including actual, potential, or perceived conflicts of interest. Afterward, when reporting the results of the external assessment, the CAE typically confirms the qualifications and independence of the external assessor or assessment team. Any actual, potential, or perceived conflicts of interest should be reported to senior management and the board. Implementation Guide 1312—External Assessments provides additional details regarding qualification and independence of external assessors.

Conclusion of Assessors

External assessment reports include the expression of an opinion or conclusion on the results of the external assessment. In addition to concluding on the internal audit activity's overall degree of conformance with the *Standards*, the report may include an assessment for each standard and/or standard series. The CAE should explain the rating conclusion(s) to senior management and the board, as well as the impact from the results. An example of a rating scale that may be used to show the degree of conformance is:

- **Generally conforms**—This is the top rating, which means that an internal audit activity has a charter, policies, and processes, and the execution and results of these are judged to be in conformance with the *Standards*.

- **Partially conforms**—Deficiencies in practice are judged to deviate from the *Standards*, but these deficiencies did not preclude the internal audit activity from performing its responsibilities.

- **Does not conform**—Deficiencies in practice are judged to be so significant that they seriously impair or preclude the internal audit activity from performing adequately in all or in significant areas of its responsibilities.

Corrective Action Plans

During an external assessment, the assessor may provide recommendations to address areas that were not in conformance with the *Standards*, as well as opportunities for improvement. The CAE should communicate to senior management and the board any action plans to address recommendations from the external assessment. The CAE may also consider adding the external assessment recommendations and action plans to the internal audit activity's existing monitoring processes related to internal audit engagement findings (see Standard 2500—Monitoring Progress). After recommendations identified during the external assessment have been implemented, the CAE generally communicates this to the board, either as part of the internal audit activity's monitoring progress or by following up separately through the next internal assessment (Standard 1311), as part of the QAIP.

Considerations for Demonstrating Conformance

Multiple items may indicate conformance with Standard 1320, including board meeting minutes or minutes from other meetings to document the discussions with senior management and the board related to the scope and frequency of both internal and external assessments. Minutes from board or other meetings should also provide documentation to support the qualifications and independence of the external assessor or assessment team. Additionally procurement documentation may show the process related to any bidding requirements to obtain services.

Other documentation may indicate conformance with the standard, specifically related to the communication of periodic internal and external assessments. Internal audit communications may include a copy of the external assessment report. This report typically provides the details that support the assessor's conclusion, and may include a rating for each standard. The external assessor may provide a presentation to senior management and the board, or the CAE may communicate the QAIP results directly.

▶ Standard 1321 – Use of "Conforms with the *International Standards for the Professional Practice of Internal Auditing*"

Indicating that the internal audit activity conforms with the *International Standards for the Professional Practice of Internal Auditing* is appropriate only if supported by the results of the quality assurance and improvement program.

Interpretation:

The internal audit activity conforms with the Code of Ethics and the Standards *when it achieves the outcomes described therein. The results of the quality assurance and improvement program include the results of both internal and external assessments. All internal audit activities will have the results of internal assessments. Internal audit activities in existence for at least five years will also have the results of external assessments.*

▶ IG1321 – Use of "Conforms with the *International Standards for the Professional Practice of Internal Auditing*"

Getting Started

Both internal and external assessments of the internal audit activity are performed to evaluate, and express an opinion on, the internal audit activity's conformance with the *International Standards for the Professional Practice of Internal Auditing* (*Standards*) and The IIA's Code of Ethics. They may also include recommendations for improvement.

The chief audit executive (CAE) should have an understanding of the requirements for a quality assurance and improvement program (QAIP) and be familiar with the results from recent internal and external assessments of the internal audit activity. The CAE typically also has an understanding of the board's expectations regarding use of the statement "Conforms with the *International Standards for the Professional Practice of Internal Auditing*." The CAE may discuss such usage with the board periodically to gain and maintain an understanding of the board's expectations on the matter.

Considerations for Implementation

Internal auditors may only communicate—in writing or verbally—that the internal audit activity conforms with the *Standards* if results of the QAIP, including both the internal and external assessment results, support such a statement. Once an external assessment validates conformance with the *Standards*, the internal audit activity may continue to use the statement—as long as internal assessments continue to support such a statement—until the next external assessment.

The following scenarios demonstrate proper use of the conformance statement:

- If the results of either the current internal assessment or most recent external assessment do not confirm general conformance with the *Standards* and the Code of Ethics, the internal audit activity must discontinue indicating that it is operating in conformance.

- If an internal audit activity has been in existence at least five years and has not completed an external assessment, the internal audit activity may not indicate that it is operating in conformance with the *Standards*.

- If an internal audit activity has undergone an external assessment within the past five years, but has not conducted an internal assessment based on disclosures to the board on the frequency of internal assessment, the CAE should consider whether it is still operating in conformance and if appropriate to indicate conformance until validated by an internal assessment.

- An internal audit activity that has been in existence fewer than five years may indicate that it is operating in conformance with the *Standards* only if a documented internal assessment (i.e., the periodic self-assessment) supports that conclusion.

- If it has been more than five years since the last external assessment was conducted in accordance with Standard 1312—External Assessments, the internal audit activity must cease indicating that it operates in conformance, until a current external assessment is completed and supports that conclusion.

- If an external assessment reflects an overall conclusion that the internal audit activity was not operating in conformance with the *Standards*, the internal audit activity must immediately discontinue using any statements that indicate conformance with the *Standards*. The internal audit activity may not resume use of a conformance statement until it has remediated the nonconformance and conducted an external assessment to validate an overall assessment of conformance with the *Standards*.

It is important to note that the *Standards* are principles-based. In assessing conformance with the *Standards*, there may be situations where the internal audit activity achieves only partial conformance with one or more standards. The internal audit activity may demonstrate a clear intent and commitment to ultimately achieving the Core Principles for the Professional Practice of Internal Auditing, on which the *Standards* are based, but may have some improvement opportunities to achieve full conformance with the *Standards*. In such cases, the internal audit activity should consider the overall conformance conclusion when determining its ability to use the conformance statement.

In a situation where a specific engagement fails to achieve conformance with the *Standards*, the internal audit activity may be required to disclose the lack of conformance. The CAE is responsible for disclosing such instances of nonconformance. Implementation Guide 1322—Disclosure of Nonconformance provides additional information about nonconformance with the *Standards*.

Considerations for Demonstrating Conformance

Multiple items may indicate conformance with Standard 1321, including copies of internal and external assessments wherein the assessor concludes that the internal audit activity has achieved conformance with the *Standards*. Engagement reports, the internal audit charter, board materials and meeting minutes, and other communications, may also help demonstrate conformance with this standard.

IG1322 – Disclosure of Nonconformance

Getting Started

The chief audit executive (CAE) is responsible for ensuring that the internal audit activity undergoes ongoing monitoring, periodic self-assessments, and independent external assessments, as required by the quality assurance and improvement program. These internal and external assessments are performed, in part, to evaluate and express an opinion regarding the internal audit activity's conformance with *International Standards for the Professional Practice of Internal Auditing* (*Standards*) and The IIA's Code of Ethics. The CAE should be familiar with the results from recent internal and external assessments of the internal audit activity.

Standard 1322 is applicable in instances where the CAE concludes that the internal audit activity does not conform with the *Standards* and the Code of Ethics, and the lack of conformance may impact the overall scope or operation of the internal audit activity. It is important that the CAE has an understanding of the mandatory elements of the International Professional Practices Framework, how potential conformance deviations might affect the overall scope of the internal audit activity, and the expectations of the board and senior management for reporting any such conformance issues.

Considerations for Implementation

The results of any internal and external assessments, and the level of internal audit conformance with the *Standards*, must be communicated to senior management and the board at least annually. These assessments may uncover impairments to independence or objectivity, scope restrictions, resource limitations, or other conditions that may affect the internal audit activity's ability to fulfill its responsibilities to stakeholders. Such nonconformance is typically reported to the board when identified and recorded in meeting minutes.

> ### ▶ Standard 1322 – Disclosure of Nonconformance
>
> When nonconformance with the Code of Ethics or the *Standards* impacts the overall scope or operation of the internal audit activity, the chief audit executive must disclose the nonconformance and the impact to senior management and the board.

If an internal audit activity fails to undergo an external assessment at least once every five years, for example, it would be unable to state that it conforms with the *Standards* (see Implementation Guide 1321—Use of "Conforms with the *International Standards for the Professional Practice of Internal Auditing*"). In such a case, the CAE would evaluate the impact of this nonconformance.

Other common examples of nonconformance may include, but are not limited to, situations in which:

- An internal auditor was assigned to an audit engagement, but did not meet individual objectivity requirements (see Standard 1120—Individual Objectivity).

- An internal audit activity undertook an engagement without having the collective knowledge, skills, and experience needed to perform its responsibilities (see Standard 1210—Proficiency).

- The CAE failed to consider risk when preparing the internal audit plan (see Standard 2010—Planning).

In such cases, the CAE would need to evaluate the nonconformance and determine whether it impacts the overall scope or operation of the internal audit activity. It is also important for the CAE to consider whether, and how much, a nonconformance situation may affect the internal audit activity's ability to fulfill its professional responsibilities and/or the expectations of stakeholders. Such responsibilities may include the ability to provide reliable assurance on specific areas within the organization, to complete the audit plan, and to address high-risk areas.

After such consideration, the CAE will disclose the nonconformance, as well as the impact of the nonconformance, to senior management and the board. Often, disclosures of this nature involve a discussion with senior management and communication to the board during a board meeting. The CAE may also discuss nonconformance during private sessions with the board, one-on-one meetings with the board chair, or by other appropriate methods.

Considerations for Demonstrating Conformance

To demonstrate conformance with Standard 1322, the internal audit activity should maintain documentation of the occurrence and nature of any nonconformance with the *Standards* or the Code of Ethics. Other items that may indicate conformance with Standard 1322 include documentation that supports the determination of overall impact of nonconformance, board meeting minutes where the internal audit activity's nonconformance with the the Code of Ethics or the *Standards* was reported, or memos or emails to senior management and the board that discuss such nonconformance. This may include the results of any internal or external assessments completed, as well as any communications that document the lack of conformance and its impact on the scope or operation of the internal audit activity.

Standard 2000 – Managing the Internal Audit Activity

The chief audit executive must effectively manage the internal audit activity to ensure it adds value to the organization.

Interpretation:

The internal audit activity is effectively managed when:

- *It achieves the purpose and responsibility included in the internal audit charter.*
- *It conforms with the* Standards.
- *Its individual members conform with the Code of Ethics and the Standards.*
- *It considers trends and emerging issues that could impact the organization.*

The internal audit activity adds value to the organization and its stakeholders when it considers strategies, objectives, and risks; strives to offer ways to enhance governance, risk management and control processes; and objectively provides relevant assurance.

(Continued on next page)

IG2000 – Managing the Internal Audit Activity

Getting Started

This standard communicates the minimum criteria that the chief audit executive (CAE) must fulfill in managing the internal audit activity. Reviewing the requirements related to each element in the Interpretation may help the CAE prepare to implement this standard.

As this standard indicates, the CAE is responsible for managing the internal audit activity in a way that enables the internal audit activity as a whole to conform with the *Standards* and individual internal auditors to conform with the *Standards* and the Code of Ethics. Thus, it is crucial that the CAE regularly reviews the International Professional Practices Framework (IPPF) to address the details of conformance.

Standard 2000 points out several fundamentals needed to fulfill the principle that the internal audit activity adds value to the organization. The CAE may start by reviewing the internal audit activity's purpose and responsibility, which is agreed upon by the CAE, senior management, and the board and recorded in the internal audit charter. Studying the organizational chart can help the CAE identify the organization's stakeholders, structure, and reporting relationships. Studying the organization's strategic plan will give the CAE insight into the organization's strategies, objectives, and risks. The risks considered should include trends and emerging issues, such as those involving the organization's industry, the internal audit profession itself, regulatory requirements, and political and economic situations. The CAE may gather additional input by speaking with senior management and the board about the strategic plan.

This forethought and preparation lays the groundwork for the CAE to manage the internal audit activity in a way that adds value by enhancing the organization's governance, risk management, and control processes and by providing relevant assurance.

Considerations for Implementation

After considering the aforementioned information, the CAE develops an internal audit strategy and approach that aligns with the goals and expectations of the organization's leadership. In addition, as stated in Standard 2010, the CAE creates a risk-based internal audit plan to determine the priorities of the internal audit activity's assurance and consulting engagements. This process takes into account the input of senior management and the board as well as a documented annual risk assessment (Standard 2010.A1).

In the internal audit plan, the CAE typically defines the internal audit activity's scope and deliverables, specifies the resources needed to achieve the plan, and outlines an approach to develop the internal audit activity and measure its performance and progress against the plan. According to Standard 2020, the CAE is responsible for communicating the plan, resource requirements, and the impact of resource limitations to the board and senior management and receiving their approval. Significant interim changes to the plan must also be communicated and approved.

As stated in Standard 2030, the CAE must also ensure that internal audit resources are deployed effectively to achieve the approved plan. To implement a systematic and disciplined approach to managing the internal audit activity, the CAE considers the Mandatory Guidance of the IPPF and establishes internal audit policies and procedures (Standard 2040). Internal audit policy and procedure documents often are assembled into an internal audit manual for the internal audit activity to use. The documents may include methods and tools for training internal auditors. The CAE may require internal auditors to acknowledgement by signature that they have read and understood the policies and procedures.

Standard 2000 introduces the CAE's responsibility for ensuring that the internal audit activity adds value to the organization by objectively providing relevant assurance and offering suggestions to enhance the organization's governance, risk management, and control processes. The 2100 series of standards and

---

(Continued)

The chief audit executive must establish a risk-based plan to determine the priorities of the internal audit activity, consistent with the organization's goals.

Interpretation:

To develop the risk-based plan, the chief audit executive consults with senior management and the board and obtains an understanding of the organization's strategies, key business objectives, associated risks, and risk management processes. The chief audit executive must review and adjust the plan, as necessary, in response to changes in the organization's business, risks, operations, programs, systems, and controls.

implementation guides describes the requirements and processes that enable the internal audit activity to complete these objectives.

The CAE ensures effective management by monitoring conformance with the Mandatory Guidance of the IPPF at both the level of the individual internal auditor and the internal audit activity as a whole. The CAE is also responsible for implementing a quality assurance and improvement program, as required by Standard 1300, and for implementing the methods and tools related to the 1200 series of standards.

The CAE must also evaluate the internal audit activity's effectiveness to achieve conformance with Standard 2000. Typically, the CAE develops metrics for evaluating the efficiency and effectiveness of the internal audit activity. Tools the CAE may use for this purpose include soliciting feedback through post-audit client surveys, completing annual performance reviews of individual internal auditors, implementing the quality assurance and improvement program, and comparing the organization's internal audit activity against contemporary internal audit groups in the industry (benchmarking).

Considerations for Demonstrating Conformance

Evidence of how well the internal audit activity has been managed and whether it has added value to the organization exists in the results of post-engagement client surveys and other sources of feedback. In addition, internal and external assessments help gauge the internal audit activity's conformance with the Mandatory Guidance of the IPPF, including performance metrics related to managing the internal audit activity. The results of comparisons against the industry standard (i.e., benchmarking) may also be used.

Because Standard 2000 requires evidence of conformance not only at the level of the internal audit activity, but also at the level of the individual internal auditor, evidence that supports the 1200 series of standards may also be useful. This may include supervisory evaluations and peer reviews of individual internal auditors and the CAE, with metrics tied to performance and conformance.

Evidence of conformance with the 2000 series of standards (i.e., standards 2010 through 2070) provides additional evidence of conformance with Standard 2000.

| Mission | Core Principles | Definition | Standards |

▶ Standard 2010 – Planning

The chief audit executive must establish a risk-based plan to determine the priorities of the internal audit activity, consistent with the organization's goals.

Interpretation:

To develop the risk-based plan, the chief audit executive consults with senior management and the board and obtains an understanding of the organization's strategies, key business objectives, associated risks, and risk management processes. The chief audit executive must review and adjust the plan, as necessary, in response to changes in the organization's business, risks, operations, programs, systems, and controls.

▶ IG2010 – Planning

Getting Started

The internal audit plan is intended to ensure that internal audit coverage adequately examines areas with the greatest exposure to the key risks that could affect the organization's ability to achieve its objectives. This standard directs the chief audit executive (CAE) to start preparing the internal audit plan by consulting with senior management and the board to understand the organization's strategies, business objectives, risks, and risk management processes. Thus, the CAE considers the maturity of the organization's risk management processes, including whether the organization uses a formal risk management framework to assess, document, and manage risk. Less mature organizations may use less formal means of risk management.

The CAE's preparation usually involves reviewing the results of any risk assessments that management may have performed. The CAE may employ tools such as interviews, surveys, meetings, and workshops to gather additional input about the risks from management at various levels throughout the organization, as well as from the board and other stakeholders.

Considerations for Implementation

This review of the organization's approach to risk management may help the CAE decide how to organize or update the audit universe, which consists of all risk areas that could be subject to audit, resulting in a list of possible audit engagements that could be performed. The audit universe includes projects and initiatives related to the organization's strategic plan, and it may be organized by business units, product or service lines, processes, programs, systems, or controls.

Linking critical risks to specific objectives and business processes helps the CAE organize the audit universe and prioritize the risks. The CAE uses a risk-factor approach to consider both internal and external risks. Internal risks may affect key products and services, personnel, and systems. Relevant risk factors related to internal risks include the degree of change in risk since the area was last audited, the quality of controls, and others. External risks may be related to competition, suppliers, or other industry issues. Relevant risk factors for external risks may include pending regulatory or legal changes and other political and economic factors.

To ensure that the audit universe covers all of the organization's key risks (to the extent possible), the internal audit activity typically independently reviews and corroborates the key risks that were identified by senior management. According to Standard 2010.A1, the internal audit plan must be based on a documented risk assessment, undertaken at least annually, that considers the input of senior management and the board. As noted in Glossary, risks are measured in terms of impact and likelihood.

When developing the internal audit plan, the CAE also considers any requests made by the board and/or senior management and the internal audit activity's ability to rely on the work of other internal and external assurance providers (as per Standard 2050).

Once the aforementioned information has been gathered and reviewed, the CAE develops an internal audit plan that usually includes:

- A list of proposed audit engagements (and specification regarding whether the engagements are assurance or consulting in nature).
- Rationale for selecting each proposed engagement (e.g., risk rating, time since last audit, change in management, etc.).
- Objectives and scope of each proposed engagement.
- A list of initiatives or projects that result from the internal audit strategy but may not be directly related to an audit engagement.

Although audit plans typically are prepared annually, they may be developed according to another cycle. For example, the internal audit activity may maintain a rolling 12-month audit plan and reevaluate projects on a quarterly basis. Or, the internal audit activity may develop a multi-year audit plan and assess the plan annually.

The CAE discusses the internal audit plan with the board, senior management, and other stakeholders to create alignment among the priorities of various stakeholders. The CAE also acknowledges risk areas that are not addressed in the plan. For example, this discussion may be an opportunity for the CAE to review the roles and responsibilities of the board and senior management related to risk management and the standards related to maintaining the internal audit activity's independence and objectivity (Standard 1100 through Standard 1130.C2). The CAE reflects on any feedback received from stakeholders before finalizing the plan.

The internal audit plan is flexible enough to allow the CAE to review and adjust it as necessary in response to changes in the organization's business, risks, operations, programs, systems, and controls. Significant changes must be communicated to the board and senior management for review and approval, in accordance with Standard 2020.

Considerations for Demonstrating Conformance

Evidence of conformance with Standard 2010 exists in the documented internal audit plan, as well as the risk assessment upon which the plan is based. Supporting evidence also may exist in the minutes of meetings where the CAE discussed the audit universe and risk assessment with the board and senior management. In addition, memos to file could be used to document similar conversations with individual members of management at various levels throughout the organization.

▶ IG 2020 – Communication and Approval

Getting Started

Before communicating to senior management and the board regarding the internal audit plan, the internal audit activity's resource requirements, and the impact of resource limitations, the chief audit executive (CAE) determines the resources needed to implement the plan, based on the risk-based priorities identified during the planning process (Standard 2010). Resources may include people (e.g., labor hours and skills), technology (e.g., audit tools and techniques), timing/schedule (availability of resources), and funding. A portion of resources is usually reserved to address changes to the audit plan that may arise, such as unanticipated risks that could affect the organization and requests for consulting engagements from senior management and/or the board. For example, the need for a new internal audit project may arise when new risks are introduced due to organizational divestitures or mergers, political uncertainty, or changes in regulatory requirements.

It is helpful if the CAE, the board, and senior management agree in advance on the criteria that would characterize a significant enough change to warrant discussion and on the protocol for communicating such changes. It may be helpful to record these criteria in the internal audit charter or other document.

Considerations for Implementation

The CAE usually itemizes the audits that comprise the internal audit plan and then assesses the types and quantity of resources that would be needed to accomplish each audit project. Estimates are generally based on past experience with a particular project or comparisons to a similar project. The CAE can compare the resources needed to accomplish the plan's priorities with those available to the internal audit activity to determine whether any gaps exist. This comparison can be used as a basis for determining the impact of resource limitations.

> ### ▶ Standard 2020 – Communication and Approval
>
> The chief audit executive must communicate the internal audit activity's plans and resource requirements, including significant interim changes, to senior management and the board for review and approval. The chief audit executive must also communicate the impact of resource limitations.

The CAE typically meets with individual senior executives to solicit their input regarding the proposed internal audit plan before it is formally presented to the board for approval. During the meetings, the CAE can address any concerns that senior executives may express, incorporate their feedback (as appropriate), and obtain their support. The process may involve gathering additional information about the timing of proposed audit engagements and the availability of resources. It might introduce changes that affect the scope of work. The insight the CAE acquires from these discussions helps determine whether any adjustments should be made to the internal audit plan before it is presented to the board for approval.

The CAE's presentation of the internal audit plan to the board usually occurs during a meeting, which may include senior management. The proposed internal audit plan may include:

- A list of proposed audit engagements (and specification regarding whether the engagements are assurance or consulting in nature).
- Rationale for selecting each proposed engagement (e.g., risk rating, time since last audit, change in management, etc.).
- Objectives and scope of each proposed engagement.
- A list of initiatives or projects that result from the internal audit strategy but may not be directly related to an audit engagement.

Resource limitations affect the priorities in the internal audit plan. For example, if resources are not sufficient to complete every proposed engagement in the plan, some engagements may be deferred, and some risks may go unaddressed. During the board presentation, the CAE discusses the proposed internal audit plan and the risk assessment on which it is based, indicating the risks that will be addressed, as well as any risks that cannot be addressed due to resource constraints. Board members can discuss this information and make recommendations before ultimately approving the internal audit plan.

The internal audit plan is developed with enough flexibility so that the CAE can adjust it as necessary in response to changes in the organization's business, risks, operations, programs, systems, and controls. However, the CAE must review *significant* changes to the audit plan, related rationale, and potential impact with the board and senior management to obtain their approval. Regularly scheduled quarterly or semiannual board meetings provide opportunities to review and adjust the internal audit plan.

Considerations for Demonstrating Conformance

The CAE may demonstrate conformance with Standard 2020 by keeping records of the distribution of the internal audit plan. Conformance may also be evidenced through a copy of board meeting materials that includes the internal audit plan as proposed for review and approval. Individual discussions with senior management could be documented through memos, emails, or notes made during the internal audit activity's risk assessment process. Typically, board meeting minutes contain records of the board's discussion and approval of the internal audit plan, any interim changes, and/or the impact of any resource limitations.

| Mission | Core Principles | Definition | Standards |

▶ Standard 2030 – Resource Management

The chief audit executive must ensure that internal audit resources are appropriate, sufficient, and effectively deployed to achieve the approved plan.

Interpretation:

Appropriate refers to the mix of knowledge, skills, and other competencies needed to perform the plan. Sufficient refers to the quantity of resources needed to accomplish the plan. Resources are effectively deployed when they are used in a way that optimizes the achievement of the approved plan.

▶ IG2030 – Resource Management

Getting Started

When developing the internal audit plan (Standard 2010) and reviewing it with the board and senior management (Standard 2020), the chief audit executive (CAE) considers and discusses the resources needed to accomplish the plan's priorities. To implement Standard 2030, the CAE usually begins by gaining a deeper understanding of the resources available to the internal audit activity in the board-approved internal audit plan.

The CAE may carefully consider the number of internal audit staff and productive work hours available to implement the plan within the organization's schedule constraints. Productive work hours generally exclude factors such as paid time off and time spent on training and administrative tasks. To gain an overview of the internal audit activity's collective knowledge, skills, and other competencies, the CAE may review a documented skills assessment, if available, or gather information from employees' performance appraisals and post-audit surveys.

The CAE may also want to reflect on the approved budget and consider the funds available for training, technology, or additional staffing in order to achieve the plan.

Considerations for Implementation

When allocating specific resources to the engagements identified in the approved internal audit plan, the CAE may consider how the available resources correspond with the specific skills and timing required to perform the engagements. During this process, the CAE typically works to fill any gaps that may have been identified.

To fill gaps related to the internal audit staff's knowledge, skills, and competencies, the CAE could provide training for existing staff, request an expert from within the organization to serve as a guest auditor, hire additional staff, or hire an external service provider. If the quantity of resources is insufficient to cover the planned engagements efficiently and effectively, the CAE may hire additional staff, cosource or outsource engagements, use one or more guest auditors, or develop a rotational auditing program.

When developing a schedule for internal audit engagements, the CAE considers the organization's schedule, the schedules of individual internal auditors, and the availability of auditable entities. For example, if an audit engagement needs to occur during a specific time of year, the resources needed to complete that engagement must also be available at that time. Likewise, if an auditable entity is unavailable or constrained during a certain period of the year, due to business needs, the engagement would be scheduled to avoid that period.

Because the CAE must report on the impact of resource limitations (Standard 2020) and on the internal audit activity's performance relative to its plan (Standard 2060), it is important for the CAE to gauge the overall adequacy of resources continuously. To affirm that resources are appropriate, sufficient, and effectively deployed, the CAE establishes metrics that assess the internal audit activity's performance and solicits feedback from internal audit clients.

Considerations for Demonstrating Conformance

Documentation that evidences conformance with Standard 2030 could include the internal audit plan, which contains the estimated schedule of audit engagements and resources allocated. Additionally, a post-audit comparison of budgeted hours to actual hours may be documented to validate that resources were deployed effectively. The results of client assessments related to the performance of the internal audit activity and individual internal auditors are often noted in post-audit reports, surveys, and annual reports.

▶ Standard 2040 – Policies and Procedures

The chief audit executive must establish policies and procedures to guide the internal audit activity.

Interpretation:

The form and content of policies and procedures are dependent upon the size and structure of the internal audit activity and the complexity of its work.

▶ IG2040 – Policies and Procedures

Getting Started

To establish the policies and procedures that guide the internal audit activity, the chief audit executive (CAE) considers several factors. It is essential to ensure that internal audit policies and procedures are aligned with the Mandatory Guidance of the International Professional Practices Framework (IPPF). Additionally, alignment with the internal audit charter helps ensure that stakeholder expectations are addressed.

The CAE may begin to develop policies and procedures by gathering information, examples, and templates, such as those available through The IIA. Templates can be customized to fit the organization and the needs of the specific internal audit activity.

It is important for the CAE to consider the organization's existing strategies, policies, and processes, including whether organizational leadership expects to review and/or approve internal audit policies and procedures.

Considerations for Implementation

The CAE's implementation of Standard 2040 will depend largely on the structure, maturity, and complexity of the organization and the internal audit activity. While a large, mature internal audit activity may have a formal internal audit operations manual that includes the policies and procedures, a smaller or less mature organization may not. Instead, policies and procedures may be published as separate documents or integrated as part of an audit management software program.

The following topics are generally included in an internal audit manual or otherwise documented to help guide the internal audit activity:

- Internal audit policies.
    - The overall purpose and responsibilities of the internal audit activity.

- Adherence to the Mandatory Guidance of the IPPF.
- Independence and objectivity.
- Ethics.
- Protecting confidential information.
- Record retention.

- Internal audit procedures.
  - Preparing a risk-based audit plan.
  - Planning an audit and preparing the engagement work program.
  - Performing audit engagements.
  - Documenting audit engagements.
  - Communicating results/reporting.
  - Monitoring and follow-up processes.

- Quality assurance and improvement program.
- Administrative matters.
  - Training and certification opportunities.
  - Continuing education requirements.
  - Performance evaluations.

To ensure internal audit personnel are properly informed about internal audit policies and procedures, the CAE may issue individual documents, training materials, or a comprehensive manual; and training sessions may be conducted to review the information. The CAE may request that internal auditors sign forms of acknowledgement, indicating that they have read and understand the policies and procedures.

Internal audit policies and procedures should be reviewed periodically, either by the CAE or an internal audit manager assigned to monitor internal audit processes and emerging issues. Such reviews may be included in the internal audit activity's internal assessments (Standard 1311) and the external assessment that occurs at least once every five years (Standard 1312).

Suggestions for operational changes may arise in response to the quality assurance and improvement program or feedback from internal auditors or audited entities (e.g., via a client satisfaction survey). If procedural changes are made, they may be communicated in writing and/or discussed during internal audit staff meetings to help ensure that the changes are understood. Training may also be conducted (e.g., to demonstrate new procedures).

Considerations for Demonstrating Conformance

Documentation of policies and procedures evidences conformance with Standard 2040. Evidence that internal audit policies and procedures have been clearly communicated to internal audit personnel may include internal audit staff meeting agendas and minutes, emails, signed acknowledgements, a training schedule, or similar documentation.

IG 2050 – Coordination and Reliance

Getting Started

The roles of assurance and consulting service providers vary by organization. Thus, to start the task of coordinating their efforts, the chief audit executive (CAE) identifies the various roles of existing assurance and consulting service providers by reviewing the organization chart and board meeting agendas or minutes. The roles are generally categorized as either internal providers or external providers.

- Internal providers include oversight functions that either report to senior management or are part of senior management. Their involvement may include areas such as environmental, financial control, health and safety, IT security, legal, risk management, compliance, or quality assurance. These are often considered "second line of defense" activities, according to The IIA's Three Lines of Defense model.

- External assurance providers may report to senior management or external stakeholders, or they could be hired by and report to the CAE.

Once the providers of assurance and consulting services have been identified, the CAE considers the type and amount of information that may be shared with them, in accordance with the organization's confidentiality requirements. It is important that the CAE considers the limitations of sharing confidential information, particularly with external parties.

Considerations for Implementation

The CAE meets with each of the providers to gather sufficient information so that the organization's assurance and consulting activities may be coordinated. Within the limitations of the organization's confidentiality requirements, the parties share the objectives, scope, and timing of upcoming reviews, assessments, and audits; the results of prior audits; and the possibility of relying on one another's work.

▶ Standard 2050 – Coordination and Reliance

The chief audit executive should share information, coordinate activities, and consider relying upon the work of other internal and external assurance and consulting service providers to ensure proper coverage and minimize duplication of efforts.

Interpretation:

In coordinating activities, the chief audit executive may rely on the work of other assurance and consulting service providers. A consistent process for the basis of reliance should be established, and the chief audit executive should consider the competency, objectivity, and due professional care of the assurance and consulting service providers. The chief audit executive should also have a clear understanding of the scope, objectives, and results of the work performed by other providers of assurance and consulting services. Where reliance is placed on the work of others, the chief audit executive is still accountable and responsible for ensuring adequate support for conclusions and opinions reached by the internal audit activity.

The process of coordinating assurance activities varies by organization. In smaller organizations, coordination may be informal. In large or heavily regulated organizations, coordination may be formal and complex.

One way to coordinate assurance coverage is to create an assurance map by linking identified significant risk categories with relevant sources of assurance and rating the level of assurance provided for each risk category. Because the map is comprehensive, it exposes gaps and duplications in assurance coverage, enabling the CAE to evaluate the sufficiency of assurance services in each risk area. The results can be discussed with the other assurance providers so that the parties may reach an agreement about how to coordinate activities to minimize duplication of efforts and maximize the efficiency and effectiveness of assurance coverage.

Another approach to coordinating assurance coverage is a combined assurance model, where internal audit may coordinate assurance efforts with second line of defense functions, such as a compliance function, to reduce the nature, frequency and redundancy of internal audit engagements.

Examples of coordinating activities include:

- Synchronizing the nature, extent, and timing of planned work.
- Ensuring a common understanding of assurance techniques, methods, and terminology.
- Providing access to one another's work programs, workpapers, and reports.
- Relying on one another's work to minimize duplication of effort.
- Meeting intermittently to determine whether it is necessary to adjust the timing of planned work, based on the results of work that has been completed.

The CAE may choose to rely on the work of other providers for various reasons, such as to assess specialty areas outside of the internal audit activity's expertise or to enhance risk coverage beyond the internal audit plan. However, if the internal audit activity relies on the work of another service provider, the CAE retains ultimate responsibility for internal audit conclusions and opinions. Thus, it is essential that the CAE establish a consistent process and set of criteria to determine whether the internal audit activity may rely on the work of another provider. In this process, the CAE may:

- Evaluate objectivity by considering whether the provider has, or may appear to have, any conflicts of interest and whether they have been disclosed.
- Consider independence by examining the provider's reporting relationships and the impact of this arrangement.
- Confirm competency by verifying whether the provider's professional experience, qualifications, certifications, and affiliations are appropriate and current.
- Assess due professional care by examining elements of the practice the provider applies to complete the work (i.e., the provider's methodology and whether the work was appropriately planned, supervised, documented, and reviewed).
- The CAE may also seek to gain an understanding of the scope, objectives, and results of the actual work performed to determine the extent of reliance that may be placed on the provider's work. The CAE typically considers whether the provider's findings appear reasonable and are based on sufficient, reliable, and relevant audit evidence. The CAE determines whether additional work or testing is needed to obtain sufficient evidence to support or increase the level of reliance desired. If additional work is needed, the internal audit activity may retest the results of the other provider.

Considerations for Demonstrating Conformance

Evidence of conformance with Standard 2050 could include communications regarding distinct assurance and consulting roles and responsibilities, which may be documented in the notes from meetings with individual providers of assurance and consulting services or in minutes of meetings with the board and senior management. Conformance with the requirements regarding reliance on the work of other providers may also be evidenced through the CAE's documentation of the process and criteria applied to determine whether the internal audit activity may rely on a provider's work. Conformance with the requirement to coordinate the providers of assurance and consulting services is evidenced through assurance maps and/or combined internal audit plans that identify which provider is responsible for providing assurance or consulting services in each area.

IG2060 – Reporting to Senior Management and the Board

Getting Started

Communicating effectively with senior management and the board is an essential responsibility of the chief audit executive (CAE), and this standard brings together the CAE's primary reporting requirements referenced throughout the *Standards*. In implementing the *Standards* related to communication, the CAE will usually want to understand the reporting-related expectations of senior management and the board, which may be stated in the audit committee charter. The three parties typically discuss and collaboratively determine the frequency and form of internal audit reporting and the reporting schedule that is most appropriate for the organization, as well as the importance and urgency of various types of audit information. It also may be helpful to agree in advance on protocols for the CAE to report important and urgent risk or control events and the related actions to be taken by senior management and the board.

Additionally, the CAE may find it helpful to establish or review:

- The internal audit charter, including the internal audit activity's purpose, authority, responsibility.
- The internal audit plan and key performance indicators to measure the internal audit activity's progress toward accomplishing the plan.
- The quality assurance and improvement program, which gauges the internal audit activity's conformance with the Mandatory Guidance of the International Professional Practices Framework (IPPF).
- Processes for identifying significant risk and control issues.

Considerations for Implementation

While Standard 2060 allows flexibility in the frequency and content of reporting, it notes that these factors will depend on the importance of the information and

> ### Standard 2060 – Reporting to Senior Management and the Board
>
> The chief audit executive must report periodically to senior management and the board on the internal audit activity's purpose, authority, responsibility, and performance relative to its plan and on its conformance with the Code of Ethics and the *Standards*. Reporting must also include significant risk and control issues, including fraud risks, governance issues, and other matters that require the attention of senior management and/or the board.
>
> (Continued on next page)

> (Continued)
>
> **Interpretation:**
>
> *The frequency and content of reporting are determined collaboratively by the chief audit executive, senior management, and the board. The frequency and content of reporting depends on the importance of the information to be communicated and the urgency of the related actions to be taken by senior management and/or the board.*
>
> *The chief audit executive's reporting and communication to senior management and the board must include information about:*
>
> - *The audit charter.*
> - *Independence of the internal audit activity.*
> - *The audit plan and progress against the plan.*
> - *Resource requirements.*
> - *Results of audit activities.*
>
> (Continued on next page)

the urgency with which senior management and/or the board might need to act on the communications. Additionally, some standards have specific requirements regarding frequency. For instance, items that must be communicated at least annually include the internal audit activity's organizational independence (Standard 1110) and the results of ongoing monitoring of the internal audit activity's performance (Standard 1320).

To maintain and track consistent and effective communication with senior management and the board, the CAE may consider using a checklist of all reporting requirements referenced throughout the *Standards*, which would the following topics:

- The internal audit charter.
- Organizational independence of the internal audit activity.
- Internal audit plans, resource requirements, and performance.
- Results of audit engagements.
- Quality assurance and improvement program.
- Conformance with the Code of Ethics and the *Standards*.
- Significant risk and control issues, and management's acceptance of risk.

Such a checklist may include a schedule of communications and reminders about any approval requirements. Establishing a standing item on the board meeting agenda secures an opportunity for the CAE to communicate regularly.

The Internal Audit Charter

According to Standard 1000—Purpose, Authority, and Responsibility, the internal audit activity's purpose, authority, and responsibility must be formally defined in the internal audit charter. The CAE is responsible for periodically reviewing the charter and presenting it to senior management and the board for approval. The Mission of Internal Audit and the mandatory elements of the IPPF, which are acknowledged in the internal audit charter, should also be discussed, according to Standard 1010—Recognizing Mandatory Guidance in the Internal Audit Charter.

Organizational Independence of the Internal Audit Activity

The organizational independence of the internal audit activity must be confirmed to the board annually, according to Standard 1110—Organizational Independence. In addition, any interference in determining the scope of internal auditing, performing work, or communicating results—as well as the implications of such interference—must be disclosed to the board, according to Standard 1110.A1. An independent reporting relationship is essential to facilitate the CAE's ability to communicate directly with the board, as required in Standard 1111—Direct Interaction With the Board.

Internal Audit Plans, Resource Requirements, and Performance

Standard 2020—Communication and Approval and the related Implementation Guidance specifies the details of communicating the internal audit activity's plans and resource requirements. Standard 2060 adds the requirement to report the internal audit activity's performance relative to its plan. This is an opportunity for the CAE to illustrate the value enhanced and protected by the internal audit activity and the implementation of its recommendations. To quantify the level of performance, many CAEs use key performance indicators such as the percentage of the audit plan completed, percentage of audit recommendations that have been accepted or implemented, status of management's corrective actions, or average time taken to issue reports. In addition, updates on any special requests made by the board and/or senior management may be discussed during board meetings.

(Continued)

- *Conformance with the Code of Ethics and the Standards, and action plans to address any significant conformance issues.*
- *Management's response to risk that, in the chief audit executive's judgment, may be unacceptable to the organization.*

These and other chief audit executive communication requirements are referenced throughout the Standards.

Results of Audit Engagements

The 2400 series of standards covers the requirements for communicating the results of audit engagements, including the information that engagement communications must contain, the quality of that information, and the protocol in the case of errors and omissions or nonconformance with the Code of Ethics or the *Standards* that affects a specific engagement. Standard 2440—Disseminating Results discusses the CAE's responsibilities related to the final engagement communication, and Standard 2450—Overall Opinions describes the criteria for issuing an overall opinion.

Quality Assurance and Improvement Program

The 1300 series of standards cover the CAE's responsibility for developing and maintaining a quality assurance and improvement program that includes internal and external assessments. Standard 1320—Reporting on the Quality Assurance and Improvement Program lists the requirements of the CAE's communication to senior management and the board, including that this reporting must occur as the assessments are completed. However, the results of ongoing monitoring of the internal audit activity's performance, which is part of the internal assessment process, must be reported at least annually.

With regard to the external assessment of the internal audit activity, which must be conducted at least once every five years, Standard 1312—External Assessments requires the CAE to discuss with the board the qualifications and independence of the external assessor or assessment team, including any potential conflict of interest. The CAE should encourage board oversight in the external assessment to reduce perceived or potential conflicts of interest.

Conformance With the Code of Ethics and the Standards

Standard 1320—Reporting on the Quality Assurance and Improvement Program and its Implementation Guidance also describe the details of reporting on the internal audit activity's conformance with the Code of Ethics and the *Standards*.

Standard 1322—Disclosure of Nonconformance states, "When nonconformance with the Code of Ethics or the *Standards* impacts the overall scope or operation of the internal audit activity, the chief audit executive must disclose the nonconformance and the impact to senior management and the board." Standard 1322 also describes considerations for reporting nonconformance. Standard 2431—Engagement Disclosure of Nonconformance stipulates the information that must be disclosed when nonconformance impacts a specific engagement. In addition, Standard 2060 calls for the CAE to communicate action plans to address any significant issues related to conformance.

Significant Risk and Control Issues and Management's Acceptance of Risk

A primary purpose of CAE reporting is to provide assurance and advice to senior management and the board regarding the organization's governance (Standard 2110), risk management (Standard 2120), and controls (Standard 2130). An in-depth understanding of these processes can be obtained by implementing the 2100 series of standards. Standard 2060 identifies the CAE's responsibility to report significant risk and control issues that could adversely affect the organization and its ability to achieve its objectives. Significant issues are those that would require the attention of senior management and the board, which may include conflicts of interest, control weaknesses, errors, fraud, illegal acts, ineffectiveness, and inefficiency.

If the CAE believes that senior management has accepted a level of risk that the organization would consider unacceptable, the CAE should first discuss the matter with senior management. If the CAE and senior management cannot resolve the matter, Standard 2600 directs the CAE to communicate the matter to the board. If such issues are too urgent to wait until a scheduled board meeting (e.g., a major fraud), the CAE would be well advised to make arrangements to communicate sooner.

Considerations for Demonstrating Conformance

CAE discussions with senior management and the board—regarding the contents of the charter, the internal audit activity's performance relative to the audit plan, and significant risk exposures or control issues—may be documented in agendas and minutes of meetings with the board and senior management. Discussions amongst these parties may also be documented in reports and presentations with attached distribution lists. Minutes from ad hoc meetings and documentation of reports and other communications sent electronically may also demonstrate conformance with Standard 2060. Board and senior management survey results and CAE performance evaluations may contain feedback that indicates the quality and effectiveness of the CAE's communication related to this standard. The CAE may also maintain a communications checklist that documents the frequency of reporting and approval requirements.

IG2070 – External Service Provider and Organizational Responsibility for Internal Auditing

Getting Started

When an external service provider is employed by an organization to serve as its internal audit activity, it is important that the external service provider understands the 1300 series of standards and can make the organization aware of its responsibility for maintaining a quality assurance and improvement program (QAIP) that covers all aspects of the internal audit activity. The external service provider should ensure that the QAIP encompasses all aspects of internal audit operations and management, in accordance with the mandatory elements of the International Professional Practices Framework (IPPF) and best practices of the internal audit profession.

The QAIP concludes on the quality of the internal audit activity and its services within the organization and may lead to recommendations for continuous improvement. The QAIP must include ongoing monitoring, periodic self-assessments, and external assessments conducted by a qualified independent party to support conformance with the *International Standards for the Professional Practice of Internal Auditing* (*Standards*) and The IIA's Code of Ethics.

The implementation guides for the 1300 series of standards provide more information about QAIP requirements, including internal and external assessments, reporting results to the board and senior management, and use of "conforms with the *International Standards for the Professional Practice of Internal Auditing*."

Considerations for Implementation

When an organization outsources internal audit work, it is not released from the responsibility for maintaining an effective internal audit activity. Thus, even when the internal audit activity is outsourced, the organization maintains responsibility

---

> ▶ **Standard 2070 – External Service Provider and Organizational Responsibility for Internal Auditing**
>
> When an external service provider serves as the internal audit activity, the provider must make the organization aware that the organization has the responsibility for maintaining an effective internal audit activity.
>
> **Interpretation:**
>
> *This responsibility is demonstrated through the quality assurance and improvement program which assesses conformance with the Code of Ethics and the* Standards.

| Mission | Core Principles | Definition | Standards |

for ensuring that the internal audit activity performs its responsibilities effectively and efficiently and conforms with the *Standards* and that individual internal auditors conform with the *Standards* and the Code of Ethics.

A QAIP, as required by Standard 1300—Quality Assurance and Improvement Program, includes both internal and external assessments. When an organization hires an external service provider to serve as the chief audit executive (CAE), that service provider must make the organization aware that the organization is responsible for maintaining an effective internal audit activity, which includes ensuring that the QAIP includes both internal and external assessments of conformance with the *Standards*.

The CAE—or the external service provider hired to serve in the CAE's role—should ensure that the organization is aware of its responsibilities related to the QAIP. Typically, a contract (i.e., engagement letter) between the organization and the external service provider specifies the service provider's responsibilities and deliverables related to the QAIP. An external service provider hired to serve as the CAE and operate as the organization's outsourced internal audit activity may also meet with senior management and the board to discuss the organization's responsibilities and the nature and requirements of a QAIP. These requirements are articulated in the 1300 series of standards.

- **Standard 1300—Quality Assurance and Improvement Program** explains that the CAE must develop and maintain a QAIP that encompasses all aspects of the internal audit activity. Where an external service provider assumes the role of CAE, the service provider may actually develop and maintain the QAIP if this is part of the contractual agreement. However, the hiring organization still maintains ultimate responsibility for the quality of the internal audit activity.

- **Standard 1310—Requirements of the Quality Assurance and Improvement Program** stipulates that the QAIP must include both internal and external assessments.

- **Standard 1311—Internal Assessments** states that the mandatory internal assessments must include both ongoing monitoring and periodic self-assessments. Where an internal audit activity is outsourced completely to an external service provider, ongoing monitoring and periodic self-assessments may be performed by the external service provider, in accordance with the contract.

- **Standard 1312—External Assessments** explains the requirements for external assessments, including their form and frequency (at least once every five years) as well as the qualification and independence requirements for the external assessor or assessment team. It's important to note that in cases where the entire internal audit activity is outsourced to an external service provider, the scope of external assessments is based solely on the work conducted for the hiring organization. Additionally, the organization should ensure that the external assessor or assessment team selected to perform the external assessment meets independence requirements.

- **Standard 1320—Reporting on the Quality Assurance and Improvement Program** outlines the CAE's responsibilities for communicating the results of the QAIP to senior management and the board. An external service provider hired to serve as the CAE and operate as the organization's outsourced internal audit activity typically meets with the board and senior management to discuss reporting requirements and expectations.

- **Standard 1321—Use of "Conforms with the *International Standards for the Professional Practice of Internal Auditing*"** indicates that internal audit activity may only communicate—in writing or verbally—conformance with the *Standards* if results of the QAIP (including internal and external assessments) support such a statement.

- **Standard 1322—Disclosure of Nonconformance** requires the CAE—or the external service provider hired to serve as CAE—to disclose to senior management and the board any instances where the internal audit activity does not conform with the *Standards* or the Code of Ethics and the lack of conformance impacts the overall scope or operation of the internal audit activity.

Considerations for Demonstrating Conformance

Multiple documents may indicate conformance with Standard 2070. First, the contract (i.e., engagement letter) between the organization and the external service provider may offer evidence of the organization's responsibility related to maintaining a QAIP. The two primary products of these responsibilities are the documented QAIP and the results of internal and external assessments. For internal assessments, documentation typically consists of the results of ongoing monitoring efforts, as well as findings, corrective action plans, and corrective actions taken as a result of periodic internal assessments to improve conformance with the mandatory elements of the IPPF. Additionally, any documentation of actions taken to improve internal audit efficiency and effectiveness may help demonstrate conformance with the standard. For external assessments, documentation from the external assessor or assessment team, or written independent validation of a self-assessment, may be used to indicate conformance.

Agendas and minutes from meetings with senior management and the board may indicate that the external service provider communicated the organization's responsibilities related to maintaining an effective internal audit activity. Meeting records could also evidence that the CAE reported on QAIP results, as required by the *Standards*. Evidence of such communication could also include memos to file or other written documents.

IG2100 – Nature of Work

Getting Started

Conforming with Standard 2100 requires a thorough understanding of the concepts of governance, risk management, and control, as defined in the *International Standards for the Professional Practice of Internal Auditing*, as well as the individual standards that apply specifically to these concepts: Standard 2110—Governance, Standard 2120—Risk Management, and Standard 2130—Control. It is also important for the internal audit activity to have an understanding of organizational objectives.

Once this understanding has been achieved, the chief audit executive (CAE) usually interviews senior management and the board to understand the roles and responsibilities of each stakeholder with respect to governance, risk management, and control. Typically, the board is responsible for guiding the governance process, and senior management is accountable for leading risk management and control processes.

Internal auditors need to understand the business to perform meaningful evaluations and may use established governance, risk management, and control frameworks as a guide in their evaluation. In addition, internal auditors may use their knowledge, experience, and best practices to proactively highlight observed weaknesses and make recommendations for improvement.

To assist the internal audit activity in its understanding of the business strategies and risks, the CAE will typically review board and committee charters, meeting agendas and minutes, and the organization's strategic plan. The CAE will also review the organization's mission, key objectives, critical risks, and the key controls used to mitigate such risks to an acceptable level. During this review, the internal audit activity may gain insight into the definitions, frameworks, models, and processes of governance, risk management, and control used by the organization. It may also be helpful for internal auditors to understand the key organizational roles related to the three processes, which may include the chairman of the board,

> ### ▶ Standard 2100 – Nature of Work
>
> The internal audit activity must evaluate and contribute to the improvement of the organization's governance, risk management, and control processes using a systematic, disciplined, and risk-based approach. Internal audit credibility and value are enhanced when auditors are proactive and their evaluations offer new insights and consider future impact.

CEO, and other chief officers (e.g., finance, ethics, risk, compliance, human resources, IT), as well as others.

For more information on governance, risk management, and control, please see the implementation guides for standards 2110, 2120, and 2130.

Considerations for Implementation

To start implementing this standard, the CAE typically discusses with the board and senior management the requirements of the standard, roles and responsibilities, and the best strategies for the internal audit activity to evaluate and contribute to governance, risk management, and control efficiently and effectively.

The CAE may document in the internal audit charter any expectations related to the roles, responsibilities, and accountabilities of the board, senior management, and the internal audit activity. This is intended to safeguard the internal audit activity's independence by affirming that senior management and the board are responsible and accountable for governance, risk management, and control, while the internal audit activity is responsible for providing objective assurance and consulting activities related to the three processes.

To devise an appropriate strategy for assessing the organization's governance, risk management, and control processes, the CAE typically considers the level of maturity of the three processes as well as the organization's culture and the seniority of the individuals who maintain responsibility for the processes. Then, the CAE assesses the risks associated with the three processes. The CAE may use established frameworks adopted by senior management (e.g., The Committee of Sponsoring Organizations of the Treadway Commission's internal control and enterprise risk management frameworks, the King Report on Corporate Governance, or ISO 31000) to guide the assessment. During the assessment, the CAE documents and discusses with senior management any relevant observations and conclusions. The CAE also makes recommendations to strengthen the processes and may escalate significant observations to the board.

If an established framework has not been adopted to guide the organization's governance, risk management, and control processes, the CAE may consider recommending an appropriate framework to guide senior management in their pursuit of enhancing these processes.

Considerations for Demonstrating Conformance

Documentation that may demonstrate conformance with the standard includes the internal audit charter, which documents the internal audit activity's roles and responsibilities related to governance, risk management, and control. Additionally, conformance may be evidenced by the internal audit plan or minutes of meetings in which the elements of the standard were discussed among the CAE, board, and senior management. Engagement plans may demonstrate the internal audit activity's disciplined, systematic, and risk-based approach, and engagement reports may demonstrate the outcome of relevant, value-added results.

Additional evidence of conformance is described in the implementation guides for standards 2110, 2120, and 2130.

Standard 2110 – Governance

The internal audit activity must assess and make appropriate recommendations to improve the organization's governance processes for:

- Making strategic and operational decisions.
- Overseeing risk management and control.
- Promoting appropriate ethics and values within the organization.
- Ensuring effective organizational performance management and accountability.
- Communicating risk and control information to appropriate areas of the organization.
- Coordinating the activities of, and communicating information among, the board, external and internal auditors, other assurance providers, and management.

IG2110 – Governance

Getting Started

To fulfill this standard, the chief audit executive (CAE) and internal auditors start by attaining a clear understanding of the concept of governance and the characteristics of typical governance processes. They should also consider the formal definition of governance, as it appears in the glossary of the *International Standards for the Professional Practice of Internal Auditing*, and become familiar with globally accepted governance frameworks and models (e.g., The Committee of Sponsoring Organizations of the Treadway Commission's frameworks or ISO 31000).

Governance frameworks, models, and requirements vary according to organization type and regulatory jurisdictions. How an organization designs and practices the principles of effective governance also depends on factors such as its size, complexity, life cycle, maturity, stakeholder structure, and the legal requirements to which the organization is subject. The CAE's approach to assessing governance and making recommendations to management will vary based on the framework or model the organization uses.

Next, the CAE contemplates whether the current internal audit plan encompasses the organization's governance processes and addresses their associated risks. Governance does not exist as a set of independent processes and structures. Rather, governance, risk management, and control are interrelated. For example, effective governance activities consider risk when setting strategy. Equally, risk management relies on effective governance (e.g., tone at the top; risk appetite, tolerance, and culture; and the oversight of risk management). Likewise, effective governance relies on internal controls and communication to the board about the effectiveness of those controls.

The CAE may review board and committee charters, as well as meeting agendas and minutes, to gain insight into the role the board plays in the organization's governance, especially regarding strategic and operational decision-making.

The CAE may also speak with others in key governance roles (e.g., chairman of the board, top elected or appointed official in a governmental entity, chief ethics officer, human resources officer, independent external auditor, chief compliance officer, chief risk officer, etc.) to gain a clearer understanding of the organization-specific processes and assurance activities already in place. If the organization is regulated, the CAE may want to review any governance concerns identified by regulators.

An understanding of governance is the foundation for a discussion with the board and senior management about:

- The definition of governance and the nature of governance processes within the organization.
- The requirements of Standard 2110.
- The internal audit activity's role.
- Any changes to the internal audit activity's approach and plan that may improve its conformance with the standard.

This discussion will help ensure agreement and an alignment of expectations with the board and senior management about what constitutes governance, so that an appropriate internal audit plan and approach can be executed.

Considerations for Implementation

Governance processes are considered during the internal audit activity's risk assessment and audit plan development. The CAE typically identifies the organization's higher-risk governance processes, which are addressed through assurance and consulting projects described in the final audit plan. In addition, Standard 2110 specifically identifies the internal audit activity's responsibility for assessing and making appropriate recommendations to improve the organization's governance processes for:

- **Making strategic and operational decisions**—To evaluate an organization's governance processes for making strategic and operational decisions, the internal audit activity may review past audit reports as well as board meeting minutes, the board policy manual, or related governance documents, which can help provide an understanding of how such decisions are discussed and ultimately made. This review typically reveals whether established, consistent decision-making processes have been developed. In addition, interviews with departmental heads may reveal what processes led to strategic and operational decisions.

- **Overseeing risk management and control**—To determine how an organization provides oversight of its risk management and control activities, the internal audit activity typically reviews the process for conducting the annual risk assessment. The internal audit activity may also review minutes from meetings wherein risk management strategy was discussed, as well as previously conducted risk assessments, and may interview key risk management personnel such as compliance, risk, and finance officers. The information obtained can be compared to benchmarking and industry trends to ensure all relevant risks have been considered.

- **Promoting appropriate ethics and values within the organization**—To assess how an organization promotes ethics and values, both internally and among its external business partners, the internal audit activity reviews the organization's related objectives, programs, and activities. These could include mission and value statements, a code of conduct, hiring and training processes, an anti-fraud and whistleblowing policy, and a hotline and investigation process. Surveys and interviews may be used to gauge whether the organization's efforts result in sufficient awareness of its ethical standards and values.

- **Ensuring effective organizational performance management and accountability**—To evaluate how an organization ensures effective performance management and accountability, the internal audit activity could review the organization's policies and processes related to staff compensation, objective setting, and performance evaluation. The internal audit activity may also review associated measurements (e.g., key performance indicators) and incentive plans (e.g., bonuses) to determine whether they are appropriately designed and executed to prevent or detect unacceptable behavior or excessive risk-taking and to support actions aligned with the organization's strategic objectives.

- **Communicating risk and control information to appropriate areas of the organization**—To appraise how well an organization communicates risk and control information to appropriate areas, the internal audit activity could access internal reports, newsletters, relevant memos and emails, and staff meeting minutes to determine whether information regarding risks and controls is complete, accurate, and distributed timely. Surveys and interviews could be used to gauge employees' understanding of their responsibilities over risk and control processes and the impact to the organization if those responsibilities are not fulfilled. Typically, during assurance and advisory engagements, the internal audit activity also evaluates how the area under review communicates risk and control information.

- **Coordinating the activities of, and communicating information among, the board, external and internal auditors, other assurance providers, and management**—To assess an organization's ability to coordinate activities and communicate information among the various parties, the internal audit activity could identify the meetings that include these groups (e.g., board, audit committee, and finance committee) and determine how frequently they occur. Members of the internal audit activity may attend the meetings as participants or observers, and they may review the meeting minutes, work plans, and reports distributed among the groups to learn how these parties coordinate activities and communicate with each other.

Internal auditors can act in a number of different capacities to assess and recommend ways to improve governance practices. They may provide independent, objective assessments of the design and effectiveness of governance processes within the organization. In addition to—or instead of—providing assurance, internal auditors may elect to provide consulting services. This may be a preferred approach, particularly when known issues exist or the governance process is immature. Whether providing consulting or assurance services, the CAE may decide to use continuous monitoring methods, such as assigning internal auditors to observe meetings of governance-related bodies and advise them on an ongoing basis. Usually, a single audit of governance is not attempted. Rather, the internal audit activity's assessment of governance processes is likely to be based on information obtained from numerous audit assignments over time.

If an overall governance assessment is appropriate, it would take into account:

- The results of audits of the specific governance processes identified above.
- Governance issues arising from audits that are not specifically focused on governance, such as:
  - Strategic planning.
  - Risk management processes.
  - Operational efficiency and effectiveness.
  - Internal control over financial reporting.
  - Risks associated with IT, fraud, and other areas.
  - Compliance with applicable laws and regulations.
- The results of management assessments (e.g., compliance inspections, quality audits, control self-assessments).
- The work of external assurance providers (e.g., legal investigators, government auditor general offices, and public accounting firms) and regulators.
- The work of internal assurance providers, or second line of defense functions (e.g., health and safety, compliance, and quality).

- Other information on governance issues, such as adverse incidents indicating an opportunity to improve governance processes.

During the planning, evaluating, and reporting phases, internal auditors consider the potential nature and ramifications of the results and ensure appropriate communications with the board and senior management.

Considerations for Demonstrating Conformance

Conformance with Standard 2110 may be documented through separate internal audit reports on individual governance processes or an overall report on governance that includes assurance-based assessments and recommendations from consulting services. Documentation may also include the minutes of a board meeting during which the CAE discussed the internal audit activity's overall assessment of governance practices. Board meeting materials may provide evidence that the board was appropriately informed about compensation and incentive packages and that it monitored the performance of senior level executives. Statements of acknowledgment, signed by staff and business partners, demonstrate the organization's efforts to promote awareness of its ethics and values.

Mission | Core Principles | Definition | Standards

▶ Standard 2120 – Risk Management

The internal audit activity must evaluate the effectiveness and contribute to the improvement of risk management processes.

Interpretation:

Determining whether risk management processes are effective is a judgment resulting from the internal auditor's assessment that:

- *Organizational objectives support and align with the organization's mission.*
- *Significant risks are identified and assessed.*
- *Appropriate risk responses are selected that align risks with the organization's risk appetite.*
- *Relevant risk information is captured and communicated in a timely manner across the organization, enabling staff, management, and the board to carry out their responsibilities.*

The internal audit activity may gather the information to support this assessment during multiple engagements. The results of these

(Continued on next page)

▶ IG2120 – Risk Management

Getting Started

To fulfill this standard, the chief audit executive (CAE) and internal auditors start by attaining a clear understanding of risk appetite, as well as the organization's business missions and objectives. It is also important to attain a complete understanding of the organization's business strategies and the risks identified by management.

Risks may be financial, operational, legal/regulatory, or strategic in nature. The *International Standards for the Professional Practice of Internal Auditing* glossary definition of risk management should be considered, along with risk management frameworks and models published globally. Additionally, Implementation Guide 2100—Nature of Work may be helpful to attain the foundation necessary to implement Standard 2120.

As this standard tasks the internal audit activity with evaluating the effectiveness of risk management processes, internal auditors will generally attain an understanding of the organization's current risk management environment and the corrective actions in place to address prior risks. It is important to know how the organization identifies, assesses, and provides oversight for risks before internal auditors start to implement Standard 2120.

In its risk assessment, the internal audit activity would consider the organization's size, complexity, life cycle, maturity, stakeholder structure, and legal and competitive environment. Recent changes in the organization's environment (e.g., new regulations, new management staff, new organization structure, new processes, and new products) may have introduced new risks. The CAE may also review the maturity of the organization's risk management practices and determine to what extent the internal audit activity will rely on management's assessment of risk.

Finally, the internal audit activity should have in place an established process for planning, auditing, and reporting risk management issues. Internal auditors will also evaluate risk management during assurance and advisory reviews related to a specific area or process.

Considerations for Implementation

Through the implementation of Standard 2120, the CAE and the entire internal audit activity will ultimately demonstrate their understanding of the organization's risk management processes and look for opportunities for improvement. Through conversations with senior management and the board, the CAE would consider the risk appetite, risk tolerance, and risk culture of the organization. The internal audit activity should alert management to new risks, as well as risks that have not been adequately mitigated, and provide recommendations and action plans for an appropriate risk response (e.g., accept, pursue, transfer, mitigate, or avoid). Additionally, the internal audit activity should obtain sufficient information to evaluate the effectiveness of the organization's risk management processes.

By reviewing the organization's strategic plan, business plan, and policies, and having discussions with the board and senior management, the CAE can gain insight to assess whether the organization's strategic objectives support and align with its mission, vision, and risk appetite. Interviews with mid-level management may provide additional insight into the alignment of the organization's mission, objectives, and risk appetite at the business-unit level.

Internal auditors should thoroughly explore how the organization identifies and addresses risks and how it determines which risks are acceptable. The internal audit activity will typically evaluate the responsibilities and risk-related processes of the board and those in key risk management roles. To accomplish this, internal auditors may review recently completed risk assessments and related reports issued by senior management, external auditors, regulators, and other sources.

Additionally, the internal audit activity typically conducts its own risk assessments. Discussions with management and the board and a review of the organization's policies and meeting minutes will generally reveal the organization's risk appetite, allowing the CAE and the internal audit activity to align their recommended

> (Continued)
>
> *engagements, when viewed together, provide an understanding of the organization's risk management processes and their effectiveness.*
>
> *Risk management processes are monitored through ongoing management activities, separate evaluations, or both.*

risk responses. The internal audit activity may consider using an established risk management or control framework (e.g., The Committee of Sponsoring Organizations of the Treadway Commission's frameworks or ISO 31000) to assist in risk identification. To remain current on potential risk exposures and opportunities, the internal audit activity may also research new developments and trends related to the organization's industry, as well as processes that can be used to monitor, assess, and respond to such risks and opportunities.

By taking these steps, internal auditors may independently perform gap analyses to determine whether significant risks are being identified and assessed adequately, and the internal audit activity will be positioned to evaluate management's risk assessment process. When reviewing the risk management process, it is important for internal auditors to identify and discuss the risks and corresponding responses that have been chosen. For example, management may choose to accept risk, and the CAE would need to determine whether the decision is appropriate, according to the organization's risk appetite or risk management strategy. If the CAE concludes that management has accepted a level of risk that may be unacceptable to the organization, the CAE must discuss the matter with senior management and may need to communicate the matter to the board, in accordance with Standard 2600—Communicating the Acceptance of Risks. In cases where management chooses to employ a risk mitigation strategy in response to identified risks, the internal audit activity may evaluate the adequacy and timeliness of remedial actions taken, if necessary. This can be achieved via reviewing the control designs and testing the controls and monitoring procedures.

To assess whether relevant risk information is captured and communicated timely across the organization, internal auditors may interview staff at various levels and determine whether the organization's objectives, significant risks, and risk appetite are articulated sufficiently and understood throughout the organization. Typically, the internal audit activity also evaluates the adequacy and timeliness of management's reporting of risk management results. The internal audit activity may review board minutes to determine whether the most significant risks are communicated timely to the board and whether the board is acting to ensure that management is responding appropriately.

Finally, the internal audit activity should take the necessary steps to ensure that it is managing its own risks, such as audit failure, false assurance, and reputation risks. Likewise, all corrective actions should be monitored.

Considerations for Demonstrating Conformance

Documents that may demonstrate conformance with Standard 2120 include the internal audit charter, which documents the internal audit activity's roles and responsibilities related to risk management, and the internal audit plan. Additionally, conformance may be evidenced by minutes of meetings in which the elements of the standard—such as the internal audit activity's risk management recommendations—were discussed among the CAE, the board, and senior management, or meetings between the internal audit activity and relevant committees, task forces, and key senior management.

Risk assessments performed by the internal audit activity and action plans for addressing risks generally demonstrate both the evaluation and improvement of risk management processes, respectively.

| Mission | Core Principles | Definition | Standards |

> **Standard 2130 – Control**

The internal audit activity must assist the organization in maintaining effective controls by evaluating their effectiveness and efficiency and by promoting continuous improvement.

> **IG2130 – Control**

Getting Started

To fulfill this standard, the chief audit executive (CAE) and internal auditors start by attaining a clear understanding of the concept of control and the characteristics of typical control processes. They should also consider the formal definition of control, as found in the glossary of the *International Standards for the Professional Practice of Internal Auditing*, as well as Implementation Guide 2100—Nature of Work. Through conversations with senior management and the board, the CAE would consider the risk appetite, risk tolerance, and risk culture of the organization. It is important for internal auditors to understand the critical risks that could inhibit the organization's ability to achieve such objectives, and the controls that have been implemented to mitigate risks to an acceptable level.

Internal auditors may find it useful to review the results of previously completed evaluations of key controls, related action plans, and the potential effects of any recent business-related changes that may introduce new risks. Internal auditors may want to consult the organization's legal department, chief compliance officer, or other relevant parties regarding laws and regulations with which the organization must comply. It is beneficial for the internal audit activity to understand how the organization remains aware of changes in regulatory requirements and ensures compliance with them.

It is important for internal auditors to obtain a thorough understanding of the control framework(s) adopted either formally or informally by the organization and to become familiar with globally recognized, comprehensive control frameworks such as *Internal Control—Integrated Framework*, issued by The Committee of Sponsoring Organizations of the Treadway Commission. Although the components, processes, and assignment of responsibility for controls are similar amongst different frameworks, the terminology used by different frameworks may vary.

Internal auditors should also understand the responsibilities related to maintaining effective controls. Senior management typically oversees the establishment, administration, and assessment of the control system. Management is generally responsible for the assessment of controls within their respective areas. The internal audit activity provides varying degrees of assurance about the effectiveness of the control processes in place. The division of responsibility may be included in a management control policy for the organization.

Finally, the internal audit activity should have in place an established process for planning, auditing, and reporting control issues.

Considerations for Implementation

Through the implementation of the standard, the CAE and the entire internal audit activity ultimately should demonstrate an understanding of the organization's control processes, alert management to new control issues, and provide recommendations and action plans for corrective actions and monitoring. The internal audit activity should obtain sufficient information to evaluate the effectiveness of the organization's control processes.

Controls are designed to mitigate risks at the entity, activity, and transaction levels. A competent evaluation of the effectiveness of controls entails assessing the controls in the context of risks to objectives at each of those levels. A risk and control matrix may help the internal auditor facilitate such assessments. Such a matrix can assist the internal audit activity in:

- Identifying objectives and the risks to achieving them.
- Determining the significance of risks, taking into consideration the impact and likelihood.
- Ascertaining the appropriate response to significant risks (e.g. accept, pursue, transfer, mitigate, or avoid).
- Ascertaining the key controls management uses to manage risks.
- Evaluating the design adequacy of controls to help determine whether it may be appropriate to test controls for effectiveness.

- Testing controls that have been deemed adequately designed to determine whether they are operating as intended.

In employing a risk and control matrix, the internal audit activity may find it helpful to interview management; review organizational plans, policies, and processes; use walk-throughs, surveys, internal control questionnaires, and flowcharts to obtain information about control design adequacy; and utilize inspections, confirmations, continuous auditing, and data analyses to test control effectiveness.

To evaluate the efficiency of controls, the internal audit activity typically determines whether management measures and monitors the costs and benefits of controls. This would include identifying whether the resources used in the control processes exceed the benefits and whether control processes create significant business concerns (e.g., errors, delays, or duplication of efforts).

It may also be useful for internal auditors to assess whether the level of a control is appropriate for the risk it addresses. One tool that many internal auditors use to visually document the relationship is a risk and control map, which plots the risk significance against control effectiveness.

To promote continuous improvement in maintaining effective controls, the internal audit activity typically provides the board and senior management with an overall assessment or compiles the results of control evaluations accumulated from individual audit engagements. The CAE may recommend the implementation of a control framework if one is not already in place. Additionally, internal auditors may make recommendations that enhance the control environment (e.g., a tone at the top that promotes a culture of ethical behavior and a low tolerance for noncompliance).

Additional steps the internal audit activity may take to promote continuous improvement in control effectiveness include:

- Providing training on controls and ongoing self-monitoring processes.
- Facilitating control (or risk and control) assessment sessions for management.

- Helping management establish a logical structure for documenting, analyzing, and assessing the organization's design and operation of controls.

- Assisting in the development of a process for identifying, evaluating, and remediating control deficiencies.

- Helping management keep abreast of emerging issues, laws, and regulations related to control requirements.

- Monitoring technological advancements that may assist with control efficiency and effectiveness.

Considerations for Demonstrating Conformance

Documents that may demonstrate conformance with Standard 2130 include the internal audit activity's assessment and testing of controls. Such documentation typically exists in auditors' workpapers and may include:

- Minutes of meetings with relevant stakeholders whereby controls were discussed.

- Risk and control matrices and maps.

- Narratives of walk-throughs.

- Results of surveys and interviews with management.

- Results of controls testing.

Conformance may also be demonstrated through plans, reports on individual engagements, follow-up on issues raised in audit reports, and/or an overall evaluation of controls. If management maintains a proper set of operating and control procedures to communicate expected controls to staff, this may also demonstrate conformance. Continuous improvement may be evidenced in the constant updating of standard operating and control procedures to reflect the changing environment.

| Mission | Core Principles | Definition | Standards |

> **Standard 2200 – Engagement Planning**
>
> Internal auditors must develop and document a plan for each engagement, including the engagement's objectives, scope, timing, and resource allocations. The plan must consider the organization's strategies, objectives, and risks relevant to the engagement.

▶ IG2200 – Engagement Planning

Getting Started

Engagement planning is critical to effective internal auditing. It is central not only to Standard 2200, but to other standards in this series as well.

When planning an audit engagement, internal auditors typically begin with an understanding of the organization's annual internal audit plan, an awareness of the planning and discussions that led to its development (see Implementation Guide 2010—Planning), and an understanding of any significant changes affecting the organization since the audit engagement was included in the annual internal audit plan. Internal auditors also need to understand how the organization's strategies, objectives, and risks impact the internal audit engagement.

It's important for internal auditors to understand the engagement planning process used by the organization's internal audit activity, which is often described in the internal audit policies and procedures manual. Internal auditors should also attain an understanding of the engagement's scope and stakeholders' expectations and become familiar with prior audits (internal or external) or compliance reviews conducted in the area under review. Additionally, internal auditors typically familiarize themselves with the strategies, objectives, and risks related to the department, area, or process to be reviewed in the upcoming engagement. It may be helpful for internal auditors to inquire whether management has performed a risk assessment in the area under review and, if so, to understand management's opinion on the risk assessment as well as any related risks and controls in the area of the upcoming audit engagement.

Internal auditors should consider the resources needed for the engagement (see Implementation Guide 2030—Resource Management), and determine how resources can be utilized most effectively.

The implementation guides for Standard 2201—Planning Considerations; Standard 2210 –Engagement Objectives; Standard 2220—Engagement Scope; Standard

2230—Engagement Resource Allocation; and Standard 2240—Engagement Work Program provide further guidance on the engagement planning process.

Considerations for Implementation

In implementing Standard 2200, it is important for internal auditors to establish engagement objectives as a critical part of planning the engagement. To that end, internal auditors should review any recent risk assessments conducted by management, as well as the internal audit risk assessment completed during annual planning, because the engagement objectives will be linked to risks in the area under review. Other considerations include previous engagement risk assessments and audit reports for the area being reviewed. Once the risk-based objectives have been established, the scope of the audit engagement can be determined, setting the boundaries under which the internal auditors will work.

To establish the engagement objectives, internal auditors generally identify data required within the engagement scope and communicate the scope to management of the area under review, giving management adequate lead time for preparation. Internal auditors also communicate with management or other key personnel in the area under review to ensure availability of key personnel early in the process.

Throughout the engagement planning process, internal auditors typically retain documentation from discussions and conclusions reached during meetings and include such documents in the engagement workpapers. During the engagement's planning stage, internal auditors will determine the level of formality and documentation needed. The organization's internal audit policy manual may specify the steps for a formal process and include pertinent templates.

During engagement planning, internal auditors may start to develop the engagement work program, giving consideration to budgets, logistics, and the final engagement communication format. The chief audit executive typically determines how, when, and to whom the engagement's results will be communicated (see Standard 2440—Disseminating Results), as well as the level of direct supervisory needs of the audit staff, specific to the engagement plan (see

Standard 2340—Engagement Supervision). The last planning step before internal auditors start fieldwork typically involves attaining audit management's approval of the engagement work program. However, the engagement plan and engagement work program may be adjusted—subject to approval by audit management—during fieldwork when new information is obtained.

Considerations for Demonstrating Conformance

Documents that may demonstrate conformance with Standard 2200 include a documented engagement plan that covers the planning considerations, engagement scope, objectives, resource allocations, and the approved engagement work program. An internal audit policies and procedures manual may include approved documentation templates related to planning the engagement. Documentation may include notes from planning meetings that preceded the engagement, such as minutes, attendees, engagement timeframe, resources available, and other key items. Such notes are typically documented in engagement workpapers.

Additionally, communications to the engagement client regarding the upcoming engagement, such as communications that discuss engagement objectives and scope, may demonstrate conformance. Any documentation from an opening or kickoff meeting after the development of the engagement work program may also serve to show conformance with Standard 2200.

Additional evidence of conformance is described in the implementation guides for Standard 2201—Planning Considerations, Standard 2210—Engagement Objectives, Standard 2220—Engagement Scope, Standard 2230—Engagement Resource Allocation, and Standard 2240—Engagement Work Program.

IG2201 – Planning Considerations

Getting Started

Internal auditors must plan engagements carefully in order to effectively accomplish the goals and objectives set forth in the annual internal audit plan and to adhere to the organization's established policies and procedures for the internal audit activity. Engagement planning typically starts with a review of the documentation that supports the annual internal audit plan.

Internal auditors can plan effectively for an engagement if they start with an understanding of the mission, vision, objectives, risk, risk appetite, control environment, governance structure, and risk management process of the area or process under review. A preliminary survey could be a valuable tool to help internal auditors achieve a sufficient understanding of the area or process to be audited.

Developing a risk and control matrix—or reviewing an existing one—is a common practice used by internal auditors to identify the risks that may impact the objectives, resources, and/or operations of the area or process under review. The risk and control matrix may provide critical feedback on the key risks that have been identified, as well as any mitigating controls. It can also be used to identify key objectives of subprocesses within the area or process to be audited.

During engagement planning, internal auditors typically gather information regarding the audit client's policies and procedures and seek to understand any IT systems used by the area under review, along with sources, types, and reliability of information used in the process and those that will be evaluated as evidence. Internal auditors also obtain and review the results of work performed by other internal or external assurance providers and/or prior audit results from the area or process under review, if applicable.

It is important for internal auditors to determine whether new processes or conditions may have introduced new risks. Additionally, it is helpful for internal auditors to determine the preliminary resources and information needed, including the internal audit skills needed to perform the audit effectively.

▶ Standard 2201 – Planning Considerations

In planning the engagement, internal auditors must consider:

- The strategies and objectives of the activity being reviewed and the means by which the activity controls its performance.

- The significant risks to the activity's objectives, resources, and operations and the means by which the potential impact of risk is kept to an acceptable level.

- The adequacy and effectiveness of the activity's governance, risk management, and control processes compared to a relevant framework or model.

- The opportunities for making significant improvements to the activity's governance, risk management, and control processes.

Considerations for Implementation

To implement Standard 2201, it is important for internal auditors to identify, understand, and document the mission, strategic objectives, goals, KPIs, risks, and controls of the area or process to be audited. Typically, internal auditors evaluate whether the risks are managed to a tolerable level through governance, risk management, and control processes.

Internal auditors may hold discussions with the management of the area under review to understand the strategies and objectives. These discussions may be supplemented by a review of strategy papers, business plans, budgets, and minutes of meetings. Significant risks may be identified in the supporting documentation. Internal auditors can use their understanding of the business and knowledge of the environment to independently evaluate the risk factors considered by business management.

Understanding the strategies, objectives, and risks of the area or process to be audited can help internal auditors to evaluate the adequacy and effectiveness of the its governance, risk management, and control processes. Internal auditors may review the organization structure, management roles and responsibilities, management reports, and operating procedures to gain an understanding of the governance, risk management, and control processes. It is also important for internal auditors to review meeting notes during the planning phase of an engagement to determine whether any additional tests should be added to the work program.

Management may maintain process flow and controls documents to meet regulatory requirements, such as Sarbanes-Oxley (USA), Turnbull (UK), or other listing rules. Internal auditors may review such documentation to identify key controls. Thereafter, internal auditors may consider using a relevant framework or model, such as The Committee of Sponsoring Organizations of the Treadway Commission's frameworks or ISO 31000, to aid the evaluation.

During engagement planning, it is important for internal auditors to consider how the internal audit activity can add value. In this regard, internal auditors use their professional judgment, knowledge, and experience to identify opportunities for making significant improvements to the organization's governance, risk management, and control processes.

While planning an engagement, internal auditors establish the engagement's objectives and scope in conformance with Standard 2210—Engagement Objectives and Standard 2220—Engagement Scope. Doing so allows internal auditors to consider what should be tested in the process or area under review. It also enables them to prioritize the areas within the engagement scope based on the significance of the risks identified. Priority is generally determined by the likelihood of a risk occurrence and the impact that risk would have on the organization if it occurred. Risks with a higher likelihood of occurrence and the greatest impact are generally given the highest priority for testing.

In addition, internal auditors typically speak with individuals who work in the area or process under review. This can enhance understanding and lead to more effective engagement planning.

Implementation Guide 2210—Engagement Objectives and Implementation Guide 2220—Engagement Scope provide additional guidance.

Considerations for Demonstrating Conformance

Documents that may demonstrate conformance with the standard include a well-documented planning memo that shows, among other things, that internal auditors have considered the items listed in Standard 2201. Other documentation, such as notes from a walk-through, process flowcharts, workpapers, and a risk and control matrix, may also demonstrate conformance.

Additionally, internal auditors generally have documentation of any gaps they may have found between policies and procedures of the area under review, and this may serve to demonstrate conformance. The opportunities for making significant improvements to the organization's governance, risk management, and controls processes may be documented in meeting minutes, presentations, or the final communication to management.

| Mission | Core Principles | Definition | Standards |

> **Standard 2210 – Engagement Objectives**
>
> Objectives must be established for each engagement.

▶ IG2210 – Engagement Objectives

Getting Started

Standard 2210 clearly states that internal auditors must establish objectives as a part of planning for each engagement. Objectives typically are developed based on key risks that have been identified related to the area or process under review.

Generally, internal auditors begin the process of establishing engagement objectives by reviewing the planning considerations (see Implementation Guide 2201—Planning Considerations) and the annual internal audit plan to attain a complete understanding of why the engagement is being conducted and what the organization aims to achieve. Internal auditors may find it helpful to begin with an understanding of the organization's mission, vision, and short-term and long-term goals, as well as key policies and procedures and how they relate to the area or process under review. Additionally, it is important for internal auditors to attain a thorough understanding of the strategies, mission, and objectives of the area or process under review, as well as its inputs and outputs.

Prior to establishing the engagement objectives, it is helpful for internal auditors to determine whether a risk assessment was performed during the engagement's planning phase and to attain a thorough understanding of the risks of both the organization and the area or process under review. In addition, it is critical to understand the expectations of stakeholders including senior management and the board.

Considerations for Implementation

Internal auditors can formulate preliminary objectives of engagements through a review of the annual internal audit plan and prior engagement results, discussions with stakeholders, and consideration of the mission, vision, and objectives of the area or process under review. The preliminary objectives are further enhanced through risk assessment exercises to cover the governance, risk management, and controls of the area or process under review. The engagement objectives articulate what the engagement is specifically attempting to accomplish and determine the engagement scope (see Implementation Guide 2220—Engagement Scope).

Engagement objectives help internal auditors determine which procedures to perform. They also help internal auditors prioritize risk and control testing of processes and systems during the engagement. Risk and control testing generally provides assurance regarding design adequacy, operating effectiveness, compliance, efficiency, accuracy, and reporting.

It is important for internal auditors to establish objectives that have a clear purpose, are concise, and link to the risk assessment. Often, internal auditors utilize best practices and frameworks, such as The Committee of Sponsoring Organizations of the Treadway Commission's frameworks or ISO 31000, when establishing objectives to address risks and controls.

During engagement planning, it is helpful for internal auditors to develop a planning memo, where they can document the objectives, scope, risk assessment, and prioritized areas for testing. The planning memo is also an important document to communicate engagement objectives, scope, and other important background information to audit team members.

Implementation Guide 2300—Performing the Engagement provides additional guidance on how to achieve the engagement objectives.

Considerations for Demonstrating Conformance

Documents that may demonstrate conformance with Standard 2210 include the planning memo containing the engagement objectives, as well as the approved audit work program, which also lists the objectives. The engagement objectives should be articulated in the final engagement communication as well.

Additional documentation that may illustrate conformance includes supporting records for the engagement, such as meeting minutes or discussion notes from interactions with stakeholders. These documents may show how the engagement objectives were derived. Additionally, internal audit policies and procedures that describe which steps internal auditors should take during an engagement may help demonstrate conformance with Standard 2210.

▶ Standard 2220 – Engagement Scope

The established scope must be sufficient to achieve the objectives of the engagement.

▶ IG2220 – Engagement Scope

Getting Started

In implementing Standard 2220, internal auditors are tasked with establishing an engagement scope that is sufficient to achieve the engagement objectives. Because an engagement generally cannot cover everything, internal auditors must determine what will and will not be included. When internal auditors establish the engagement scope, they generally consider factors such as the boundaries of the area or process, in-scope versus out-of-scope locations, subprocesses, components of the area or process, and time frame.

Internal auditors typically review the planning considerations (see Implementation Guide 2201—Planning Considerations) and the engagement objectives (see Implementation Guide 2210—Engagement Objectives) to attain an understanding of the key risks identified during the planning phase. This allows them to achieve a thorough understanding of how best to link the engagement scope to the objectives. It is important for internal auditors to carefully consider the boundaries of the engagement, as the scope must cover enough breadth to achieve the engagement objectives.

Considerations for Implementation

During planning, internal auditors typically draft a scope statement that specifically states what will and will not be included in the engagement (e.g., the boundaries of the area or processes, in-scope versus out-of-scope locations, subprocesses, components of the area or process, and time frame). The time frame may be based on a point in time, a fiscal quarter, a calendar year, or another predetermined period of time.

To ensure the scope is sufficient to meet the engagement objectives and aligns with the organization's annual internal audit plan, internal auditors must use sound professional judgment based upon relevant experience and/or supervisory assistance. When determining the scope, it is helpful for them to review the engagement objectives to ensure that each objective can be accomplished under the established parameters. Internal auditors generally consider and document any scope limitations, as well as any requests from the client or stakeholders for items to be included or excluded from the scope. If internal auditors encounter scope limitations, these must be reported in the final engagement communication.

At times, internal auditors may place reliance on work performed by others—such as external auditors or compliance groups within the organization—and it may be useful to document such reliance in the scope statement. Standard 2050—Coordination and Reliance and its Implementation Guide provide further guidance on the internal audit activity's reliance on such work.

Considerations for Demonstrating Conformance

Documents that may demonstrate conformance with Standard 2220 include the description of engagement planning process in the internal audit charter or internal audit policies and procedures, which typically explains how the scope is defined. The engagement work program, approved by internal audit management, generally shows whether the engagement scope adequately aligns with the objectives and addresses the key risks identified.

Typically, the scope statement is clearly documented in the engagement's final communications. Other documentation that may serve to demonstrate conformance includes planning memos, signed approvals, engagement announcements, and notes from meetings during which the scope was discussed.

> ## Standard 2230 – Engagement Resource Allocation

Internal auditors must determine appropriate and sufficient resources to achieve engagement objectives based on an evaluation of the nature and complexity of each engagement, time constraints, and available resources.

Interpretation:

Appropriate refers to the mix of knowledge, skills, and other competencies needed to perform the engagement. Sufficient refers to the quantity of resources needed to accomplish the engagement with due professional care.

> ## IG2230 – Engagement Resource Allocation

Getting Started

In order to satisfy Standard 2230, internal auditors must ensure that resources are allocated to achieve the objectives of the engagement. It is critical that internal auditors assigned to an engagement possess the necessary knowledge, skills, experience, and additional competencies to perform the engagement competently and thoroughly. It is also important for the internal audit activity to include a quantity of resources sufficient to cover the needs of the engagement with the required attention to detail and professional care.

Before determining how best to allocate engagement resources, internal auditors generally attain an understanding of the engagement's objectives and scope by reviewing the planning documents. It is also essential for internal auditors to understand the nature and complexity of the engagement through discussions with key stakeholders, including management in the area to be audited.

It is important for internal auditors to inventory not only staff resources, but also available technology that may be helpful or necessary to perform a quality engagement. They may also consider whether additional outside resources or technology are necessary to complete the engagement.

By reviewing the engagement work program, internal auditors may gain a thorough understanding of how much time each step is expected to take. They should be aware of the number of hours budgeted for the engagement, as well as any time, language, logistical, or other constraints for any relevant party (e.g., members of the internal audit activity, management in the area under review, senior management, the board, and/or external parties).

If the internal audit activity does not have appropriate and sufficient resources on staff, the chief audit executive (CAE) is expected to obtain competent advice or assistance to fill any gaps. Implementation Guide 1210—Proficiency provides further guidance on obtaining the knowledge, skills, and other competencies necessary to perform internal audit responsibilities.

Considerations for Implementation

Internal auditors typically evaluate the engagement work program and use their best professional judgment in determining the type and quantity of resources to allocate to an engagement to best accomplish its objectives. It is important to assign the appropriate personnel to the engagement based on their availability, knowledge, skills, and experiences. Specialized skill sets (e.g., financial reporting, IT, cost analysis, asset disposition, construction, industry-specific skills, and others) can be invaluable to the internal audit activity if utilized properly. Therefore, it is important for internal auditors to exercise care when selecting the best available resources for the engagement.

If the specialized skills of the available internal auditors are not sufficient to perform the engagement, internal auditors typically consider whether additional training is an option, or whether closer supervision would be appropriate. In situations where the existing internal audit staff lacks the expertise or knowledge to perform the engagement, internal auditors may consider supplementing existing resources with other options, such as using guest auditors, employing a subject matter expert, or cosourcing.

Internal auditors should discuss with the CAE any concerns related to the resources allocated to the engagement. Internal auditors may consider tracking the actual time spent performing the engagement against the budgeted time. The causes for, and effects of, significant overrun may be documented as a lesson learned for future planning purposes.

Considerations for Demonstrating Conformance

Documents that may demonstrate conformance with Standard 2230 include the approved engagement work program, which typically shows that the internal audit activity utilized appropriate and sufficient resources for the engagement, including personnel with appropriate internal audit experience, skills, and competencies. The supporting documentation generally shows the distribution of activities for each internal auditor, as well as the timelines assigned to the engagement.

Other documentation that may illustrate conformance with Standard 2230 includes the internal audit activity's planning notes, which may describe the technology or other resources that were considered during the planning phase of the engagement. In addition, time sheets or tracking documentation used to monitor budgeted hours against actual hours may help to show conformance. A post-audit client survey on the quality of internal audit resources and timeliness of the audit report may also help to demonstrate conformance.

IG2240 – Engagement Work Program

Getting Started

To implement Standard 2240, internal auditors begin with a clear and thorough understanding of the engagement's objectives and scope, as well as the key risks and controls in the area or process under review. Typically, they a have a complete understanding of the resources available for the engagement.

Before developing the work program, internal auditors may find it useful to consider many aspects of the upcoming engagement, including:

- The appropriate sample size for testing and methodologies to be used.
- The risk register or risk matrix and how it applies to the development of the work program.
- The scope of the engagement.
- How engagement objectives will be achieved.
- Whether the necessary resources are available.
- Judgments and conclusions made during the engagement's planning phase.

Considerations for Implementation

When developing the work program, internal auditors generally consider the risks in the area or process under review. The work program is based on the engagement objectives and scope. It typically includes resource deployment plans and describes the techniques or methodologies that will be used to conduct the engagement (e.g., sampling techniques). It is important for internal auditors to determine which tests or audit steps are necessary to assess the risks in the area or process under review and to test the existing controls. Additionally, internal auditors should ensure that the tests are specific enough to avoid scope creep.

Standard 2240 – Engagement Work Program

Internal auditors must develop and document work programs that achieve the engagement objectives.

To develop an effective work program, internal auditors consider the nature, extent, and timing of the audit tests required to achieve the engagement objectives. Each engagement procedure in the work program should be designed to test a particular control that addresses risk. It is also important that the work program be developed and documented in such a way that ensures all members of the engagement team understand what they need to do and which tasks remain to be performed.

The format of work programs may vary by engagement or organization. Commonly used formats include standard templates or checklists to document completion of planning steps, memoranda that summarize tasks completed, and additional columns in the risk and control matrix. Well documented work programs assist in communicating roles, responsibilities, and tasks to the members of the engagement team. They may include signoff for completed work, the names of the internal auditors who completed the work, and the date the work was completed.

Per Standard 2240.A1, work programs must be approved by internal audit management before the commencement of audit fieldwork. However, with new information and knowledge gained during fieldwork, the audit program may be adjusted, subject to prompt approval by internal audit management.

Considerations for Demonstrating Conformance

The work program itself, with documented approval, generally demonstrates conformance with Standard 2240. Any changes to the work program also should have documented approval. Engagement supervision and appropriate signoffs for each work program task by the internal auditor responsible for completing the task may help demonstrate conformance as well.

Other documents that may illustrate conformance with Standard 2240 include meeting notes or memos that show planning steps for developing the work program. Additionally, notes from planning meetings with the audit engagement team during which the deliverables and purpose were discussed with the engagement client, or evidence that such meetings occurred, may demonstrate conformance.

IG2300 – Performing the Engagement

Getting Started

In the *International Standards for the Professional Practice of Internal Auditing*, the engagement process is divided into three phases, with a series of standards representing each: planning (2200 series), performing and supervising (2300 series), and communicating (2400 series). In reality, the standards in these groups are not performed discretely and sequentially. Rather, some engagement work may be performed during the planning process; and planning, supervising, and communicating occur throughout the performance of an engagement. Thus, in preparing to perform an engagement, internal auditors should review all three groups of standards and implementation guides concurrently.

Before performing the engagement, internal auditors may benefit from reviewing the information formulated during the planning process, which should include:

- Engagement objectives that reflect the results of a preliminary risk assessment conducted by the internal audit activity (Standard 2210—Engagement Objectives and Standard 2210.A1).

- The criteria that will be used to evaluate the governance, risk management, and controls of the area or process under review (Standard 2210.A3).

- The engagement work program (which contains the conclusions made during the planning phase), the engagement tasks, and the procedures that will be used to identify, analyze, and document engagement information (Standard 2240—Engagement Work Program and Standard 2240.A1).

Work performed during the planning phase is typically documented in workpapers and referenced in the work program. The work may include:

- A risk and control matrix, which links risks and controls with the testing approach, results, observations, and conclusions.

> ### Standard 2300 – Performing the Engagement
>
> Internal auditors must identify, analyze, evaluate, and document sufficient information to achieve the engagement's objectives.

- Process maps, flowcharts, and/or narrative descriptions of control processes.
- The results of evaluating the adequacy of control design.
- A plan and approach for testing the effectiveness of key controls.

The level of analysis and detail applied during the planning phase varies by internal audit activity and engagement. Evaluating the adequacy of control design is often completed as part of engagement planning, because it helps internal auditors clearly identify key controls to be further tested for effectiveness. However, the most appropriate time to perform this evaluation depends on the nature of the engagement; if it is not completed during planning, the control design evaluation may occur as a specific stage of engagement performance, or internal auditors may evaluate the control design while performing tests of the controls' effectiveness.

Considerations for Implementation

The 2300 series of standards encompasses performing the tests outlined in the planning phase and evaluating and documenting the results. As internal auditors reflect on the information needed to accomplish the engagement objectives, they should consider the expectations of the board and senior management. The type of information required and analyses applied may depend on whether the engagement is designed to provide assurance with conclusions and/or an opinion (Standard 2410.A1) or consulting and advice (Standard 2410.C1).

Internal auditors approach engagements with an objective, yet inquisitive, mind and search strategically for information (e.g., audit evidence) that could help achieve the engagement objectives. At each step in the engagement process, internal auditors apply professional skepticism to evaluate whether the information is sufficient and appropriate to provide a reasonable basis on which to formulate conclusions and/or recommendations, or whether additional information should be collected. Standard 2330—Documenting Information requires internal auditors to document information resulting from the execution of the engagement; the evidence should logically support the conclusions and engagement results.

The Interpretation of Standard 2310—Identifying Information states, "Sufficient information is factual, adequate, and convincing so that a prudent, informed person would reach the same conclusions as the auditor." Thus, engagement information should be collected and documented in such a way that a prudent, informed person, such as another internal auditor or an external assessor, could repeat the engagement and achieve an outcome that confirms the internal auditor's results and logically leads to the same conclusions.

Internal auditors must base conclusions and engagement results on appropriate analyses and evaluations (see Standard 2320—Analysis and Evaluation). For assurance engagements and some consulting engagements, the ultimate goal is to reach conclusions about whether the design and operation of key controls support the engagement subject's ability to achieve its objectives.

As part of the work program, internal auditors usually create a testing plan to gather evidence about the operating effectiveness of adequately designed key controls (see Standard 2240—Engagement Work Program). Generally, secondary controls (i.e., those that improve the process but are not essential) and controls that have a design weakness (i.e., those unlikely to accomplish their purpose even if they are operating properly) do not need to proceed to the level of effectiveness testing. If the details of the testing plan are not sufficient, internal auditors may need to provide additional testing details, such as the testing criteria and population, the sampling methodology, and the sample size needed to obtain sufficient information. Standard 2240.A1 requires adjustments to be approved promptly.

Internal auditors' approach to evaluation often includes a combination of manual audit procedures and computer-assisted audit techniques (CAATs). General categories of manual audit procedures include inquiry (e.g., interviews or surveys), observation, inspection, vouching, tracing, reperformance, confirmation, and analytical procedures (e.g., ratio analysis, trend analysis, or benchmarking). CAATs include generalized audit software programs and specialized programs that test the processing logic and controls of other software and systems. Evaluation procedures are discussed in more detail in Implementation Guide 2320—Analysis and Evaluation.

As evaluations are completed, the results may be recorded in a column added to the risk and control matrix, which is typically documented as a workpaper. Entries in the matrix generally include a reference or link to additional workpapers that document the details of testing procedures and analyses used, the results, and any additional support for the internal auditor's conclusions. Internal audit information, testing results, and the basis for conclusions may also be presented in the form of a summary of the work performed.

The chief audit executive usually establishes a common approach to workpaper documentation in the internal audit activity's policies and procedures manual. Documentation is discussed in more detail in Implementation Guide 2330—Documenting Information.

Considerations for Demonstrating Conformance

Conformance with Standard 2300 may be evidenced in the engagement workpapers that describe the actions, analyses, and evaluations performed during an engagement, as well as the logic supporting the conclusions, opinions, and/or advice. Workpapers normally include a description of any CAATs or software that was used during the engagement. Additionally, final engagement communications typically demonstrate conformance. Post-engagement surveys or other feedback mechanisms may confirm that the engagement's objectives were achieved, from the perspective of the board and senior management. Documentation of engagement supervision may provide evidence of conformance.

IG2310 – Identifying Information

Getting Started

The internal audit activity uses a systematic and disciplined approach to evaluate and improve the effectiveness of governance, risk management, and control processes. The systematic and disciplined approach requires that internal auditors identify, analyze, evaluate, and document information to support the results of an engagement and the internal auditors' conclusions. Standard 2310 defines the criteria of the information that must be identified.

Internal auditors begin gathering information, which includes audit evidence, when planning the engagement. A review of the engagement objectives and engagement work program helps prepare internal auditors to identify sufficient, reliable, relevant, and useful information. The work program prescribes the procedures internal auditors use to perform the engagement.

It may be helpful for internal auditors to review the organization's policies and jurisdictional laws related to data privacy before beginning engagement work. They may also consult with the organization's legal counsel or other applicable subject matter experts to address any questions or concerns that may arise about access to personal information.

The process of identifying information is facilitated by open and collaborative communication between the internal auditor and the organization's personnel, especially those directly involved with the area or process under review. Establishing and maintaining effective channels of communication is an important aspect of performing the engagement. Organizational independence of the internal audit activity is also essential for open communication (see Standard 1110—Organizational Independence).

Considerations for Implementation

During engagement planning, internal auditors gather information about the audit client and document the information in workpapers. The level of analysis

---

▶ Standard 2310 – Identifying Information

Internal auditors must identify sufficient, reliable, relevant, and useful information to achieve the engagement's objectives.

Interpretation:

Sufficient information is factual, adequate, and convincing so that a prudent, informed person would reach the same conclusions as the auditor. Reliable information is the best attainable information through the use of appropriate engagement techniques. Relevant information supports engagement observations and recommendations and is consistent with the objectives for the engagement. Useful information helps the organization meet its goals.

| Mission | Core Principles | Definition | Standards |

and detail applied during the planning phase varies by internal audit activity and engagement. Evaluating the adequacy of control design is often completed as part of engagement planning because it helps internal auditors identify key controls to be further tested for effectiveness. Thus, audit evidence may result from testing the design of control processes.

According to Standard 2310, the reliability of the audit information depends on the use of appropriate engagement techniques. Some techniques take longer or require more resources than others, but may be worth the investment because they enable a higher level of assurance. In general, simple manual audit procedures include:

- Inspecting physical evidence, such as the physical property of the area under review.
- Examining documentation from either the audit client or outside sources.
- Gathering testimonial evidence through interviews, surveys, or risk and control self-assessments.
- Conducting a walk-through to observe a process in action.
- Examining data that is continuously monitored via technology.

More complex procedures for analyzing and evaluating information are discussed in greater detail in Implementation Guide 2320—Analysis and Evaluation.

The sufficiency and reliability of information increase when the information is current, corroborated, and/or obtained directly by an internal auditor (e.g., observing a process or reviewing documentation) or from an independent third party. Information is also more reliable when it is gathered from a system where the controls are operating effectively.

Perhaps one of the most important characteristics of sufficient and reliable information is that it should be gathered and documented such that a prudent, informed person (e.g., an internal audit supervisor or external assessor) would be

International Professional Practices Framework

able to repeat the steps and tests described in the workpapers, achieve the same results, and logically reach the same conclusions as the original internal auditors who performed the work. Therefore, it is important that the chief audit executive (CAE) establishes a system of documentation, including preferred terminology and standardized notations (e.g., symbols and tick marks), and that internal auditors use this system consistently. Documentation is discussed in greater detail in Implementation Guide 2330—Documenting Information.

Because engagement resources are not unlimited, it is important for internal auditors to identify and prioritize the most relevant and useful information (i.e., information that supports, or gives credibility to, engagement observations and recommendations). It is also important for internal auditors to critically assess all of the engagement information as a whole, rather than relying on singular examples, as their conclusions and advice are based on evidence that is persuasive, rather than absolute.

Considerations for Demonstrating Conformance

Conformance with Standard 2310 may be evidenced in the engagement work program and the supporting engagement workpapers, which may be stored electronically or in paper format. Workpapers are usually organized in the order of the work program and link to the work program, whether they exist as individual pages or audit steps in a computerized audit system. As a result of supervision, evidence to support objectives is achieved through identification of sufficient, reliable, relevant, and useful information.

To confirm that the information provided was useful to the organization, surveys could be issued to personnel in the area under review (after audit engagement communications are completed). In addition, the CAE monitors the disposition of the engagement results communicated to management, which may provide evidence of the usefulness of the information communicated.

> **Standard 2320 – Analysis and Evaluation**
>
> Internal auditors must base conclusions and engagement results on appropriate analyses and evaluations.

▶ IG2320 – Analysis and Evaluation

Getting Started

While planning the engagement, internal auditors must develop a work program to achieve the engagement objectives (see Standard 2240—Engagement Work Program). For assurance engagements, the work program must include the procedures for identifying, analyzing, evaluating, and documenting engagement information (Standard 2240.A1). The 2300 series of standards describes the actual implementation of these planned procedures.

Standard 2320 requires internal auditors to analyze and evaluate the information obtained during the engagement before drawing conclusions. When planning the engagement and creating the work program, internal auditors may have completed several engagement steps and generated important information, including a risk and control matrix and an evaluation of the adequacy of control design. The work program often links to workpapers that document the work completed, information produced, and resulting decisions. Examples of typical workpapers include: a planning memorandum or checklist, flowcharts or narrative descriptions of key processes, a process-level risk map, and a risk and control matrix that documents the links between risks, controls, the testing approach, summaries of interviews, results, evidence, and conclusions.

Considerations for Implementation

The transition from planning to performing an engagement may not be completely distinct, because both phases involve some degree of analyzing and evaluating audit information. Often during the planning process, internal auditors identify controls and evaluate the adequacy of their design, because this helps them identify key controls to be tested further for effectiveness.

Performing the engagement generally involves conducting the tests prescribed in the work program to gather evidence about the operating effectiveness of key controls. Based on the risk and control matrix and work program, internal auditors are likely to have a list of specific procedures and tests to be conducted. Other factors that are usually established in the work program include management assertions; testing objectives, criteria, approach, procedures, and population; and sampling methodology and sample sizes. However, some details may still need to be determined in the early stages of performing the engagement.

Ultimately, internal auditors seek to reach conclusions as a result of executing the work program (e.g., a conclusion about whether controls are effective in mitigating risks to an acceptable level). With sufficient information about both the design adequacy and the operating effectiveness of controls, internal auditors can conclude on whether existing controls are adequate to help achieve the objectives of the area or process under review.

The extent of testing depends on whether test results have produced sufficient audit evidence on which internal auditors can base their conclusions or advice. If the testing procedures prescribed in the work program do not provide sufficient information to make conclusions and recommendations, internal auditors may need to adjust the testing plan and perform additional testing. Standard 2240.A1 requires adjustments to the work program to be approved promptly.

Analyses

Testing approaches often include a combination of manual audit procedures and computer-assisted audit techniques (CAATs); the latter includes generalized auditing software programs and programs that specialize in testing the processing logic and controls of other software and systems. Like the testing information described previously, the engagement testing procedures are usually determined during the development of the engagement work program (Standard 2240).

Internal auditors may test a complete population or a representative sample of information. If they choose to select a sample, they are responsible for applying methods to assure that the sample selected represents the whole population and/or time period to which the results will be generalized. The use of CAATs may enable the analysis of an entire population of information, rather than just a sample. Additional details about sampling techniques and CAATS may be found in The IIA's Supplemental Guidance.

Simple manual audit procedures include gathering information through inquiry (e.g., interviews or surveys), observation, and inspection. Other manual audit procedures may take longer to conduct, but generally provide a higher level of assurance. Examples of manual audit procedures include:

- Vouching—Internal auditors test the validity of documented or recorded information by following it backward to a tangible resource or a previously prepared record.

- Tracing—Internal auditors test the completeness of documented or recorded information by tracking information forward from a document, record, or tangible resource to a subsequently prepared document.

- Reperformance—Internal auditors test the accuracy of a control by reperforming the task, which may provide direct evidence of the control's operating effectiveness.

- Independent confirmation—Internal auditors solicit and obtain written verification of the accuracy of information from an independent third party.

Analytical procedures are used to compare information against expectations, based on an independent (i.e., unbiased) source and the premise that certain relationships between information can be reasonably expected in the absence of conditions to the contrary. Analytical procedures may also be used during engagement planning (2200 series of standards). Examples of analytical procedures include:

- Ratio, trend, and regression analysis.
- Reasonableness tests.
- Period-to-period comparisons.

- Forecasts.
- Benchmarking information against similar industries or organizational units.

Internal auditors may further investigate any significant deviations from the expectations to determine the cause and/or reasonableness of the variance (e.g., fraud, error, or a change in conditions). Unexplainable results may indicate a need for additional follow-up and may suggest the presence of a significant problem that should be communicated to senior management and the board (see Standard 2060—Reporting to Senior Management and the Board).

Evaluations

Internal auditors apply their experience, logic, and professional skepticism to evaluate the information discovered throughout the engagement and reach logical conclusions. Internal auditors generally approach engagements with an objective and inquisitive mind, searching strategically for information that could fulfill the engagement objectives. At each step in the engagement process, they apply professional experience and professional skepticism to evaluate whether evidence is sufficient and appropriate to formulate conclusions and/or recommendations. According to Standard 2330—Documenting Information, internal auditors must document information that logically supports the engagement results and conclusions. However, this does not mean that internal auditors should exclude relevant information that may contradict the conclusions.

Internal auditors often conduct a root cause analysis to identify the underlying reason for the occurrence of an error, problem, missed opportunity, or instance of noncompliance. Root cause analyses enable internal auditors to add insights that improve the effectiveness and efficiency of the organization's governance, risk management, and control processes. However, these analyses also sometimes require extensive resources, such as time and subject matter expertise. Thus, when conducting a root cause analysis, internal auditors must exercise due professional care by considering effort in relation to the potential benefits (Standard 1220.A1).

Although complex issues may require more rigorous analyses, in certain circumstances a root cause analysis may be as simple as asking a series of "why" questions in an attempt to identify the root cause of a variance. For example:

The worker fell. Why? Because oil was on the floor. Why? Because a part was leaking. Why? Because the part keeps failing. Why? Because the quality standards for suppliers are insufficient.

Most root causes can be traced back to decisions, actions, or inactions by a person or multiple people. However, determining a true root cause may be difficult and subjective, even after internal auditors have performed an analysis of quantitative and qualitative data. In some cases, multiple errors with varying degrees of influence may combine to form the root cause of an issue, or the root cause could involve a risk related to a broader issue such as the organizational culture. Therefore, internal auditors may choose to include input from several internal and external stakeholders. In some cases, internal auditors may provide a variety of possible root causes for management to consider, based on an independent and objective evaluation of various scenarios as the root cause of an issue. When the time frame or skill levels needed to complete the root cause analysis exceed that which is available within the internal audit activity, the chief audit executive may recommend that management address the underlying issue and conduct further work to identify the root cause.

Considerations for Demonstrating Conformance

Workpapers generally document sufficient information about the engagement's analyses, results, and conclusions to enable the reader to understand the basis of the conclusions. Workpapers also typically describe the test population, sampling process, and sampling method that the internal auditors used. Workpapers are cross-referenced in the work program. Supervisory reviews of the engagement (Standard 2340—Engagement Supervision) may provide additional validation.

IG2330 – Documenting Information

> **Standard 2330 – Documenting Information**
>
> Internal auditors must document sufficient, reliable, relevant, and useful information to support the engagement results and conclusions.

Getting Started

Engagement workpapers are used to document the information generated throughout the engagement process, including planning; testing, analyzing, and evaluating data; and formulating engagement results and conclusions. Workpapers may be maintained on paper, electronically, or both. Use of internal audit software may enhance consistency and efficiency.

The content, organization, and format of workpapers generally vary by organization and the nature of the engagement. However, it is important to achieve workpaper consistency within the internal audit activity as much as possible, as it generally helps facilitate sharing of engagement information and coordination of audit activities. Because the chief audit executive (CAE) is responsible for such coordination and for developing the internal audit activity's policies and procedures (see Standard 2050—Coordination and Reliance and Standard 2040—Policies and Procedures, respectively), it is logical for the CAE to develop guidelines and procedures for completing workpapers for various types of engagements. The use of standardized, yet flexible, workpaper formats or templates, improves the efficiency and consistency of the engagement process. Commonly standardized workpaper elements include the general layout, "tick-mark" notation (i.e., symbols used to represent specific audit procedures), a system of cross-referencing to other workpapers, and designated information that should be saved permanently or carried forward into other engagements. Before documenting engagement information, internal auditors should review and understand their organization's particular workpaper development procedures, standardized notations, and any available templates or software that the internal audit activity uses.

Considerations for Implementation

Standard 2310—Identifying Information states, "Internal auditors must identify sufficient, reliable, relevant, and useful information to achieve the engagement's objectives." These characteristics are equally essential for internal auditors to consider when documenting information in workpapers. Effective workpapers contain information that is sufficient and relevant to the engagement objectives, observations, conclusions, and recommendations, which makes the information useful in helping the organization meet its goals.

The information documented in effective workpapers is also reliable because it is derived using appropriate engagement techniques, which are documented. Perhaps most importantly, workpapers contain sufficient and relevant information that would enable a prudent, informed person, such as another internal auditor or an external auditor, to reach the same conclusions as those reached by the internal auditors who conducted the engagement. Thus, workpaper documentation is an important part of a systematic and disciplined engagement process because it organizes audit evidence in a way that enables reperformance of the work and supports engagement conclusions and results.

Workpapers may include the following elements:

- Index or reference number.
- Title or heading that identifies the area or process under review.
- Date or period of the engagement.
- Scope of work performed.
- Statement of purpose for obtaining and analyzing the data.
- Source(s) of data covered in the workpaper.
- Description of population evaluated, including sample size and method of selection.
- Methodology used to analyze data.
- Details of tests conducted and analyses performed.
- Conclusions including cross-referencing to the workpaper on audit observations.

- Proposed follow-up engagement work to be performed.
- Name of the internal auditor(s) who performed the engagement work.
- Review notation and name of the internal auditor(s) who reviewed the work.

Generally, workpapers are organized according to the structure developed in the work program and cross-referenced to relevant pieces of information. The end result is a complete collection of documentation (electronic, paper, or both) of the procedures completed, information obtained, conclusions reached, recommendations derived, and the logical basis for each of the steps. This documentation constitutes the primary source of support for internal auditors' communication with stakeholders, including senior management, the board, and management of the area or process under review.

The supervisory review of workpapers is typically used to develop internal audit staff (see Standard 2340—Engagement Supervision). A supervisory review may also be used as a basis for assessing conformance with the International Standards for the Professional Practice of Internal Auditing and for maintaining the quality assurance and improvement program (see Standard 1300—Quality Assurance and Improvement Program).

Considerations for Demonstrating Conformance

Properly prepared and completed workpapers, whether stored on paper or electronically, demonstrate conformance with Standard 2330. Evidence that the engagement information is sufficient, reliable, relevant, and useful may be demonstrated in management's effective implementation of recommended actions. When communicating engagement results to the appropriate parties, the CAE may also receive feedback about the quality of the engagement information documented. Similarly, post-engagement surveys of the individuals who received the engagement information may also evidence conformance.

Standard 2340 – Engagement Supervision

Engagements must be properly supervised to ensure objectives are achieved, quality is assured, and staff is developed.

Interpretation:

The extent of supervision required will depend on the proficiency and experience of internal auditors and the complexity of the engagement. The chief audit executive has overall responsibility for supervising the engagement, whether performed by or for the internal audit activity, but may designate appropriately experienced members of the internal audit activity to perform the review. Appropriate evidence of supervision is documented and retained.

IG2340 – Engagement Supervision

Getting Started

The chief audit executive (CAE) has overall responsibility for supervising engagements to ensure that objectives are achieved, quality is assured, and staff is developed. Thus, when planning how the engagement will be supervised, the CAE should review the engagement objectives and the internal audit policies and procedures that support fulfillment of Standard 2340. Even before the engagement planning process begins, the CAE usually has developed internal audit policies and procedures to address how engagements are planned, performed, and supervised (see Standard 2040—Policies and Procedures). Such policies and procedures may specify software programs or templates that internal auditors should use to establish consistent formats for work programs and workpapers. Similarly, policies and procedures may address opportunities for staff development, such as a policy requiring post-engagement meetings between the internal auditor(s) who performed the engagement and the CAE or designated engagement supervisor.

Skills assessments of the internal audit staff are ongoing, not solely as part of the engagement process. Skills assessments generally provide sufficient information about the internal auditors' competencies to enable the CAE to appropriately assign internal auditors to engagements for which they possess the required knowledge, skills, and other competencies. Likewise, they enable the CAE to designate a qualified engagement supervisor.

Considerations for Implementation

Engagement supervision is a process that begins with engagement planning and continues throughout the engagement. During the planning phase, the engagement supervisor is responsible for approving the engagement work program and may assume responsibility for other aspects of the planning process (see Standard 2240.A1). The primary criterion for approval of the work program is whether it is designed to achieve the engagement objectives efficiently. Additionally, the work program must include procedures for identifying, analyzing, evaluating, and documenting engagement information. Standard 2240.A1 states that any adjustments to the work program must be approved. Engagement supervision also involves ensuring that the work program is completed and authorizing any changes to the work program.

The engagement supervisor typically maintains ongoing communication with the internal auditor(s) assigned to perform the engagement and with management of the area or process under review. The engagement supervisor usually reviews the engagement workpapers that describe the audit procedures performed, the information identified, and the observations and preliminary conclusions made during the engagement. The supervisor evaluates whether the information, testing, and results are sufficient, reliable, relevant, and useful to achieve the engagement objects and support the engagement results and conclusions, as required by Standard 2330—Documenting Information.

Standard 2420—Quality of Communications requires engagement communications to be accurate, objective, clear, concise, constructive, complete, and timely. Engagement supervisors review engagement communications and workpapers for these elements, because workpapers provide the primary support for engagement communications.

Throughout the engagement, the engagement supervisor and/or CAE meet with the internal auditor(s) assigned to perform the engagement and discuss the engagement process, which provides opportunities for training, development, and evaluation of the internal auditor(s). When reviewing the engagement communications and engagement workpapers, which document all aspects of the engagement process, supervisors may ask for additional evidence or clarification. Internal auditors may have an opportunity to improve their work by answering questions posed by the engagement supervisor.

Usually, the supervisor's review notes are cleared from the final documentation once adequate evidence has been provided or workpapers have been amended with additional information that addresses the concerns and/or questions raised by the supervisor. Another option is for the internal audit activity to retain a separate record of the engagement supervisor's concerns and questions, the steps taken to resolve them, and the results of those steps.

The CAE is responsible for all internal audit engagements and all significant professional judgments made throughout the engagements, whether by the internal audit activity or others performing the work for the internal audit activity. Therefore, the CAE usually develops policies and procedures designed to minimize the risk that internal auditors will make judgments or take actions that are inconsistent with the CAE's professional judgment and could adversely affect the engagement. The CAE usually establishes a means for resolving any professional judgment differences that may arise. This may include discussing pertinent facts, pursuing additional inquiry or research, and documenting and concluding on the differing viewpoints in engagement workpapers. If there is a difference in professional judgment over an ethical issue, the issue may be referred to those individuals in the organization who have responsibility over ethical matters.

Considerations for Demonstrating Conformance

Evidence of conformance with Standard 2340 may include engagement workpapers, either initialed and dated by the engagement supervisor (if documented manually) or electronically approved (if documented within a workpaper software system). Additional evidence may include a completed engagement workpaper review checklist and/or a memorandum of review comments.

The assurance of engagement-level quality may also be demonstrated through the CAE's maintenance of a quality assurance and improvement program and through the results of surveys soliciting feedback about the engagement experience from the individuals directly involved with the engagement. Internal auditors may have the opportunity to provide feedback about the engagement supervisor through peer review mechanisms, such as surveys.

IG 2400 – Communicating Results

Getting Started

The standard requires internal auditors to communicate engagement results. Therefore, internal auditors must have a clear understanding of engagement communication requirements. The chief audit executive (CAE) also should understand the expectations of the board and senior management regarding communication related to engagement results.

Internal auditors should understand the policies and procedures in the audit manual—or any other stakeholder expectations—and the use of any standard templates to ensure consistency in developing observations and conclusions. Standard 2040—Policies and Procedures, and the related Implementation Guide, provide more information about the CAE's responsibilities related to policies and procedures.

Considerations for Implementation

Typically, the internal audit policies and procedures manual establishes the process for documenting the support for an observation/conclusion related to the engagement. The internal audit activity may develop an engagement communication plan to provide detailed guidance on how internal auditors will communicate observations during the engagement, and how they will communicate final engagement results.

In communicating results, internal auditors consider the communication plan, including criteria for communicating (Standard 2410), the quality of the communications (Standard 2420), and the dissemination of results (Standard 2440). After determining that these communication standards have been met, the internal auditor confirms how the results of the engagement will be communicated. The workpapers will indicate which results will be communicated verbally, and which will be communicated in writing.

> ### Standard 2400 – Communicating Results
>
> Internal auditors must communicate the results of engagements.

Considerations for Demonstrating Conformance

Documentation that may demonstrate conformance with Standard 2400 includes an internal audit policies and procedures manual that contains:

- Policies regarding the communication of noncompliance with laws, regulations, or other issues.
- Policies for communicating sensitive information within and outside the chain of command.
- Policies for communicating outside the organization.

Other documentation might include a communication plan, observation and escalation records, interim and preliminary communication documents, final engagement communication documents, and monitoring and follow-up communication documents.

IG2410 – Criteria for Communicating

> **Standard 2410 – Criteria for Communicating**
>
> Communications must include the engagement's objectives, scope, and results.

Getting Started

Engagement communications are a critical component of how an internal audit activity demonstrates value. The format and content of such communications may vary by organization or type of engagement.

Communicating to stakeholders requires careful planning. It is helpful to develop a plan for communicating about the engagement, and to discuss and agree upon the plan with stakeholders in advance, if possible.

To ensure criteria for communications are met, the internal audit activity must be aware of Standard 2200—Engagement Planning, Standard 2210—Engagement Objectives, Standard 2220—Engagement Scope, Standard 2300—Performing the Engagement, Standard 2310—Identifying Information, Standard 2320—Analysis and Evaluation, Standard 2330—Documenting Information, and Standard 2340—Engagement Supervision. Engagement scope and objectives are typically communicated:

- During engagement planning.
- During the engagement, if there are deviations to the planned scope and objectives.
- In the final engagement communication.

Adequate supervision ensures that the engagement's scope and objectives are achieved and appropriate controls are in place related to the quality communication of results.

Considerations for Implementation

It is important to consider the communication plan for an engagement at, or near, the commencement of the engagement. Typically, the plan addresses why, what, to whom, and how internal auditors will communicate. For example, internal auditors will communicate the objectives, scope, interim results, and final results of the engagement. The plan may also specify the use of a particular communication format. (The decision process around what should and should not be reported formally will be documented in the engagement's workpapers.) The communication plan is typically discussed with relevant stakeholders, such as those responsible for the area under review, in advance of any engagement fieldwork. The plan may be updated periodically if circumstances require a change.

When planning the final engagement communication, internal auditors will consider any initial discussions and interim communications they may have had with management of the area under review. They will carefully review all relevant workpapers and workpaper summaries and consider several additional factors, including:

- Stakeholder expectations.
- Engagement objectives.
- Strategic goals of the area under review.
- Scope of the engagement and any scope limitations.
- Engagement results.

Internal auditors should also consider the Standard 2410.A1 requirement to include in the final engagement communication applicable conclusions, as well as applicable recommendations and/or action plans. Opinions at the engagement level may include a rating, conclusion, or other description of the results and their significance, as further explained in the Interpretation of Standard 2410.A1.

Communication with management is an ongoing process throughout the engagement. The internal audit activity adds value by developing communications (both verbal and written) that effect positive change in the organization. When communicating engagement results, internal auditors are encouraged to acknowledge satisfactory performance and include any statements on limitations of distribution and/or use of the results, as communicated in Standard 2410.A2 and Standard 2410.A3.

Considerations for Demonstrating Conformance

Materials that may demonstrate conformance with Standard 2410 include written internal audit activity policies and procedures that address consistency of the engagement report format and any materials—such as records, internal memos, or email correspondence—that demonstrate how the final communication plan was developed. Conformance may be demonstrated through adherence to the communication plan or evidenced by a written report (and its appropriate content), workpapers, and/or minutes from meetings where issues and results were discussed.

An engagement letter or the internal audit activity's report on initial client meetings may demonstrate conformance, as they usually outline the engagement's work program, objectives, and scope, as well as the agreed-upon parameters of the final communication. A final report that includes the engagement objectives, scope, and results, as well as applicable conclusions with recommendations and/or action plans, may also demonstrate conformance. The final report may acknowledge satisfactory performance and any limitations related to communication or use of results to parties outside of the organization.

| Mission | Core Principles | Definition | Standards |

▶ Standard 2420 – Quality of Communications

Communications must be accurate, objective, clear, concise, constructive, complete, and timely.

Interpretation:

Accurate communications are free from errors and distortions and are faithful to the underlying facts. Objective communic ations are fair, impartial, and unbiased and are the result of a fair-minded and balanced assessment of all relevant facts and circumstances. Clear communications are easily understood and logical, avoiding unnecessary technical language and providing all significant and relevant information. Concise communications are to the point and avoid unnecessary elaboration, superfluous detail, redundancy, and wordiness. Constructive communications are helpful to the engagement client and the organization and lead to improvements where needed. Complete communications lack nothing that is essential to the

(Continued on next page)

▶ IG2420 – Quality of Communications

Getting Started

Communication occurs throughout the engagement. Therefore, Standard 2420 is applicable at all stages of the engagement, including planning and performing the engagement, communicating results, monitoring progress, and communicating the acceptance of risk. Because high-quality engagement communications are critical, internal auditors pay great attention to detail when drafting communications and consider the characteristics of quality communications outlined in the Interpretation of Standard 2420.

To ensure conformance with Standard 2420, internal auditors should understand the organization's expectations for communication, including stakeholder expectations regarding communication deadlines. These typically are addressed by a pre-established communication plan, as explained in Implementation Guide 2410—Criteria for Communicating.

Internal auditors may review the internal audit activity policies and procedures, which are often compiled in an internal audit manual, to identify any templates that should be used; templates generally help ensure proper, consistent communication during all phases of the engagement. Reviewing the writing style guidelines used by the organization before drafting the final communication may help internal auditors present the final communication in alignment with the organization's accepted writing style.

Considerations for Implementation

The Interpretation of Standard 2420 defines specific characteristics of quality communications: accurate, objective, clear, concise, constructive, complete, and timely. Internal auditors may consider the following additional information related to each:

- **Accurate**—The Interpretation notes that accurate communications are free from errors and distortions and faithful to the underlying facts. To maintain accuracy, it is important to use precise wording supported by evidence gathered during the engagement. Additionally, according to The IIA's Code of Ethics, internal auditors are required to "disclose all material facts known to them that, if not disclosed, may distort the reporting of activities under review." If an error in communications does occur, the chief audit executive (CAE) must communicate the corrected information, as described in Standard 2421—Errors and Omissions.

- **Objective**—To ensure objectivity in communications, internal auditors use unbiased phrasing and focus on deficiencies in processes and their execution. Objectivity begins with the unbiased mental attitude that internal auditors should possess when performing engagements. Objectivity is an ethical principle described in The IIA's Code of Ethics and Standard 1120—Individual Objectivity. The Core Principles for the Professional Practice of Internal Auditing also highlight the importance of objectivity and specify that for an internal audit activity to be considered effective, the internal auditors and the internal audit activity should be objective and free from undue influence (independent).

- **Clear**—Clarity in communications is increased when internal auditors use language that is easily understood by the intended audience and is consistent with terminology used in the industry and by the organization. Furthermore, clear communications avoid unnecessary technical language. The Interpretation of Standard 2420 also points out that clear communications are logical, a hallmark of the systematic, disciplined, and risk-based approach of internal audit work. As such, clarity is enhanced when internal auditors communicate important observations and findings and logically support recommendations and conclusions for a particular engagement.

- **Concise**—Internal auditors ensure that communications are appropriately concise by avoiding redundancies and excluding information that is unnecessary, insignificant, or unrelated to the engagement.

- **Constructive**—It is helpful for internal auditors to use a constructive tone throughout the communication that reflects the severity of the

> (Continued)
>
> *target audience and include all significant and relevant information and observations to support recommendations and conclusions. Timely communications are opportune and expedient, depending on the significance of the issue, allowing management to take appropriate corrective action.*

observations. Constructive communications enable a collaborative process for determining solutions that facilitate positive change in the subject of the engagement and/or the organization. Ultimately, as indicated by the Definition of Internal Auditing, internal auditors seek to help the organization accomplish its objectives.

- **Complete**—To ensure completeness of communications, it is helpful for internal auditors to consider any information essential to the target audience. Complete written communications generally enable the reader to reach the same conclusion as the internal audit activity did.

- **Timely**—Finally, it is important that internal auditors submit all communications by the deadlines established during the planning phase. Timeliness may be different for each organization. To determine what is timely, internal auditors often benchmark and conduct other research relative to the engagement subject. Additionally, the CAE or the internal auditor may establish key performance indicators that measure timeliness.

Considerations for Demonstrating Conformance

Materials that may demonstrate conformance with Standard 2420 include final communication documents approved by the chief audit executive, as well as supporting documents. Internal auditors should be able to show that such documents align with the final communication plan. In the case of communications that occur without a written report, meeting minutes may provide evidence of conformance.

IG2421 – Errors and Omissions

Getting Started

The chief audit executive (CAE) should understand the expectations of the board and senior management regarding which errors or omissions they would consider significant. Significance is defined in the glossary of the *International Standards for the Professional Practice of Internal Auditing* as "the relative importance of a matter within the context in which it is being considered, including quantitative and qualitative factors, such as magnitude, nature, effect, relevance, and impact. Professional judgment assists internal auditors when evaluating the significance of matters within the context of relevant objectives."

Considerations for Implementation

If the CAE becomes aware of an error or omission in the final engagement communication, he or she may consider the following questions to help determine its significance:

- Would the error or omission change the results of the engagement?
- Would the error or omission change someone's mind about the severity of the findings?
- Would the error or omission change a conclusion?
- Would the error or omission change an opinion?
- Would the error or omission change a recommended action?

If the answer to any of the above questions is "yes," the CAE may determine that the error or omission is significant. The CAE usually attempts to find the cause of the error or omission to prevent a similar situation from occurring in the future and to determine whether the cause needs to be included in the communication to senior management and the board. The CAE then determines the most appropriate method of communication to ensure the corrected information is received by all

> ### Standard 2421 – Errors and Omissions
>
> If a final communication contains a significant error or omission, the chief audit executive must communicate corrected information to all parties who received the original communication.

parties who received the original communication. Communicating effectively about errors and omissions and their causes serves to protect the integrity and status of the internal audit activity.

Considerations for Demonstrating Conformance

Conformance with Standard 2421 may be demonstrated by the existence of internal audit policies and procedures for handling errors and omissions. Email correspondence and other records may document how the CAE determined the significance and cause of the error or omission.

Evidentiary materials—such as the CAE's calendar, board or other meeting minutes where an error or omission was discussed, internal memos, and email correspondence—may show the specific information that was communicated as well as how and when the communication occurred. Finally, the original and corrected final communication documents evidence conformance.

IG2430 – Use of "Conducted in Conformance with the *International Standards for the Professional Practice of Internal Auditing*"

> **Standard 2430 – Use of "Conducted in Conformance with the *International Standards for the Professional Practice of Internal Auditing*"**
>
> Indicating that engagements are "conducted in conformance with the *International Standards for the Professional Practice of Internal Auditing*" is appropriate only if supported by the results of the quality assurance and improvement program.

Getting Started

To conform with Standard 2430, the chief audit executive (CAE) should understand the requirements related to developing and maintaining a quality assurance and improvement program (QAIP) (the 1300 series of standards) and be familiar with the results of the internal audit activity's current internal and external assessments. The CAE may also consider the board's expectations for using the statement "conducted in conformance with the International Standards for the Professional Practice of Internal Auditing" in engagement reports.

Considerations for Implementation

When an internal audit activity reports on an engagement, there is no requirement to indicate whether the engagement was conducted in conformance with the *International Standards for the Professional Practice of Internal Auditing (Standards)*. However, using this statement builds the internal audit activity's credibility. Standard 2430 prohibits using the statement unless the results of the internal audit activity's QAIP—including current internal and external assessments—support a conclusion that the internal audit activity generally conforms with the *Standards*. Implementation Guide 1300—Quality Assurance and Improvement Program provides additional guidance about QAIP requirements.

When an internal audit activity does not conform with the Standards, the internal audit activity may choose to state that the engagement was not conducted in conformance with the Standards. However, such a statement is not required.

Considerations for Demonstrating Conformance

When engagement reports include the statement "conducted in conformance with the *International Standards for the Professional Practice of Internal Auditing*," the results of the QAIP often are sufficient to demonstrate conformance with Standard 2340. The internal audit activity's determination of whether to use the statement in final communications may be documented in an engagement report template or other engagement communication records and/or internal audit policies and procedures. Comprehensive review of such documents would indicate whether the statement was used appropriately. Conversely, the internal audit activity may choose not to include a conformance statement in any engagement reports, and documentation of this decision is also acceptable as evidence of conformance with Standard 2430.

IG2431 – Engagement Disclosure of Nonconformance

Getting Started

Standard 2431 requires disclosure when the results of a specific engagement are impacted by nonconformance with the Code of Ethics or the *Standards*. Therefore, internal auditors should have an understanding of the Code of Ethics and the *Standards*. They should also understand the potential areas of nonconformance at the engagement level and the expectations of senior management and the board for reporting any nonconformance issues.

The Code of Ethics comprises broad principles relevant to the profession and practice of internal auditing and more specific rules of conduct, which describe the behavior expected of both entities and individuals who perform internal audit services in accordance with the Definition of Internal Auditing (including IIA members, recipients of IIA certifications, and certification candidates). The purpose of the Code of Ethics is to promote an ethical culture in the global profession of internal auditing.

As stated in the Introduction to the *Standards*, "The purpose of the *Standards* is to:

1. Guide adherence with mandatory elements of the International Professional Practices Framework.
2. Provide a framework for performing and promoting a broad range of value-added internal auditing services.
3. Establish the basis for the evaluation of internal audit performance.
4. Foster improved organizational processes and operations.

"The *Standards* are a set of principles-based, mandatory requirements consisting of:

- Statements of core requirements for the professional practice of internal auditing and for evaluating the effectiveness of performance that are internationally applicable at organizational and individual levels.
- Interpretations clarifying terms or concepts within the *Standards*."

> ### Standard 2431 – Engagement Disclosure of Nonconformance
>
> When nonconformance with the Code of Ethics or the Standards impacts a specific engagement, communication of the results must disclose the:
>
> - Principle(s) or rule(s) of conduct of the Code of Ethics or *Standard*(s) with which full conformance was not achieved.
> - Reason(s) for nonconformance.
> - Impact of nonconformance on the engagement and the communicated engagement results.

Considerations for Implementation

At times, certain circumstances may prevent internal auditors from conforming with the Code of Ethics or the *Standards* during the performance of an engagement. In general, these are circumstances in which the independence and/or objectivity of an internal auditor is impaired, or an internal auditor encounters unreliable data, a lack of information, a scope limitation, or other constraints. In such cases, the internal auditor should identify any principles, rules of conduct, or standards with which full conformance was not achieved and determine whether the nonconformance impacts the engagement results. If the nonconformance does affect the results, the engagement communications would describe why the nonconformance occurred and how the results and communications were affected.

It may be helpful to contemplate several scenarios in which Standard 2431 would apply:

- In a situation where an impairment to an internal auditor's objectivity or independence is found to impact engagement results, the communication of results must disclose nonconformance with Standard 1120—Individual Objectivity and the Code of Ethics principle of objectivity.

- In a situation where the internal audit activity undertook an engagement for which it did not possess the collective knowledge, skills, and experience needed to perform its responsibilities, the communication of results must disclose nonconformance with Standard 1210 -- Proficiency and the Code of Ethics principle of competence.

- If the internal audit activity encounters any restrictions in its ability to access records, personnel, or properties, and these restrictions impact the scope of the engagement, the communication of results must disclose nonconformance with Standard 2220.A1.

- If internal audit resources are insufficient to achieve engagement objectives, the communication must disclose nonconformance with Standard 2230—Engagement Resource Allocation.

Disclosures of this nature are typically documented in engagement workpapers. It is important for the CAE to consider whether the nonconformance situations affect the internal audit activity's ability to fulfill its professional responsibilities and/or meet the expectations of shareholders. Then, the CAE would determine how and whether to communicate these issues to senior management and the board. Often, disclosures are handled through a discussion with senior management and are communicated to the board during a meeting. The CAE may discuss nonconformance in advance during a private meeting with the board, one-on-one meeting with the chair, or by another appropriate method. To ensure full disclosure, the CAE should also consider whether the nonconformance should be included in the final engagement communication.

Considerations for Demonstrating Conformance

Materials that may demonstrate conformance with Standard 2431 include:

- Written department policies and procedures for disclosing nonconformance with the Code of Ethics and/or the *Standards* in the engagement workpapers.

- Memos, emails, or other written communications that identify Code of Ethics principles or rules of conduct and standards with which conformance was not achieved; explain the reason(s) for nonconformance; and describe the impact of nonconformance on the engagement and the communicated engagement results.

- Minutes of meetings or other records documenting verbal disclosure of the nonconformance, reason(s) for nonconformance, and the impact of nonconformance on the engagement and the communicated engagement results.

- Evidence of disclosure in the final engagement communication.

Mission Core Principles Definition Standards

▶ Standard 2440 – Disseminating Results

The chief audit executive must communicate results to the appropriate parties.

Interpretation:

The chief audit executive is responsible for reviewing and approving the final engagement communication before issuance and for deciding to whom and how it will be disseminated. When the chief audit executive delegates these duties, he or she retains overall responsibility.

▶ IG2440 – Disseminating Results

Getting Started

Standard 2440 states the chief audit executive's (CAE's) responsibility for communicating final results to all appropriate parties following an engagement. When preparing to implement this standard, the CAE may find it helpful to review the requirements related to each element in the Interpretation.

The CAE will typically have an understanding of any organizational communication protocols as well as the organization chart. The CAE should also consider the expectations of senior management and the board related to engagement communications.

The audit charter and communication protocols of the organization may help the CAE determine the process for reporting outside the organization. Considerations would include factors such as which parties to address or copy in the final communication and when to notify regulators who oversee the organization's industry.

The implementation guides for Standard 2400—Communicating Results, Standard 2410—Criteria for Communicating, and Standard 2420—Quality of Communications provide further guidance on communicating engagement results.

Considerations for Implementation

Through discussions with the board and review of any organizational communication protocols, the CAE determines who will receive the results from the engagement and what form the communications will take. Before communicating the results, it can be advantageous for the CAE to review the draft engagement communication(s).

When determining the recipients of the report, the CAE may take into consideration whether any parties have a business need for receiving the results, as well as whether any have responsibility for management action plans. Consideration may be given to organizational protocols to ensure individuals at the appropriate level of responsibility receive a copy of the report. Senior management and the board may be included in the distribution, as per their expectations. To ensure consistency, the internal audit activity may develop a standard distribution list of parties who will receive all communications, as well as management levels that should be included on a distribution list for engagement results pertaining to their area of responsibility. However, the CAE may expand that distribution list when necessary, which will often include senior management of the organization.

Results may be communicated verbally or in writing, and the format may differ depending on the recipient. The CAE determines which format to use for each recipient. For example, some recipients may receive an executive summary, while others will receive a full report. It may be appropriate for results to be delivered via a meeting with a presentation and an opportunity for discussion. Regardless of the method of communication, the CAE should determine who will deliver and receive the results.

The final communication(s) require the approval of the CAE or a designee of the CAE. In a small internal audit activity, the CAE may prepare the final engagement communication(s) personally. However, in larger organizations, the CAE will obtain and review the communication(s), and determine how much reliance to place on the internal auditor who prepared the report before giving final approval.

The CAE may deliver electronic and/or hard copies of the final engagement communications to the appropriate internal and external parties, as agreed upon in the planning phase of the engagement, and/or as required by the audit charter and communication protocols. Typically, the recipients are parties who can address the results of the engagement.

Maintaining a complete list of recipients of internal audit engagement results is important in the event that an error or omission is identified after the dissemination of results. Standard 2421 addresses the CAE's responsibility for communicating an error or omission.

To ensure compliance with legal obligations and organizational protocols, it is important for the CAE to take great care and consideration when preparing to disseminate results outside of the organization. In addition, the CAE should consider the ramifications of communicating sensitive information, as such information might impact the organization's market value, reputation, earnings, or competitiveness. The CAE may find it helpful to consult with legal counsel and compliance areas within the organization.

It's important to note that the CAE may delegate the authority for implementing Standard 2440, but responsibility cannot be delegated. When the authority for implementing Standard 2440 is delegated, the CAE maintains responsibility and accountability.

Considerations for Demonstrating Conformance

The CAE can demonstrate conformance with Standard 2440 by verifying the level of review and ensuring sign-off on all workpapers before issuing the final communication(s). In addition, retained copies of any written communication of results—by management, the audit committee, the CEO, outside parties, or others—may demonstrate conformance. Evidence of verbal communication of results may be maintained through meeting minutes, presentations, and memos that identify attendees receiving the communication. It is important to keep records that verify the CAE's approval of the final communication(s) and delivery of engagement results to recipients identified in the communication plan.

IG2450 – Overall Opinions

Getting Started

An overall opinion is the rating, conclusion, and/or other description of results provided by the chief audit executive (CAE) when addressing—at a broad level—governance, risk management, and/or control processes of the organization. An overall opinion is the professional judgment of the CAE based on the results of a number of individual engagements and other similar activities—such as reviews by other assurance providers—for a specific time interval.

Overall opinions differ from conclusions in that a conclusion is drawn from one engagement, and an overall opinion is drawn from multiple engagements. Also, a conclusion is part of an engagement communication, while an overall opinion is communicated separately from engagement communications.

The Interpretation of Standard 2310—Identifying Information defines the terms sufficient, reliable, relevant, and useful:

- Sufficient information is factual, adequate, and convincing so that a prudent, informed person would reach the same conclusions as the internal auditor.
- Reliable information is the best attainable information through the use of appropriate engagement techniques.
- Relevant information supports engagement observations and recommendations and is consistent with the objectives for the engagement.
- Useful information helps the organization meet its goals.

The Interpretation of Standard 2450 points out the required components for a communication of an overall opinion; the CAE should understand all of these components before issuing an overall opinion. Additionally, the CAE should have a good understanding of the organization's strategies, objectives, and risks as well as the expectations of the board and senior management prior to issuing an overall opinion.

Standard 2450 – Overall Opinions

When an overall opinion is issued, it must take into account the strategies, objectives, and risks of the organization; and the expectations of senior management, the board, and other stakeholders. The overall opinion must be supported by sufficient, reliable, relevant, and useful information.

Interpretation:

The communication will include:

- *The scope, including the time period to which the opinion pertains.*
- *Scope limitations.*
- *Consideration of all related projects, including the reliance on other assurance providers.*
- *A summary of the information that supports the opinion.*
- *The risk or control framework or other criteria used as a basis for the overall opinion.*
- *The overall opinion, judgment, or conclusion reached.*

The reasons for an unfavorable overall opinion must be stated.

Considerations for Implementation

The CAE starts by considering how an opinion will relate to the strategies, objectives, and risks of the organization. The CAE further considers whether the opinion will solve a problem, add value, and/or provide management or other stakeholders with confidence regarding an overall trend or condition in the organization. Discussions with senior management, the board, and other relevant stakeholders may help the CAE understand the expectations for the scope of the overall opinion.

The CAE then determines the scope of the overall opinion to be provided, including the time period to which the opinion relates, and considers whether there are any scope limitations. With this information in mind, the CAE can determine which audit engagements would be relevant to the overall opinion. All related engagements or projects are considered, including those completed by other internal and external assurance providers. Internal assurance providers may include other functions that comprise the second line of defense for the organization. External service providers may include the work of external auditors or regulators. For each project considered from an internal or external assurance provider, the CAE will need to assess the project to determine the level of reliance that can be placed on the project work. If the CAE relies on the work of another assurance provider, the CAE still retains responsibility for the overall opinion that was reached as a result of that reliance.

For example, an overall opinion may be based on aggregate engagement conclusions at the organization's local, regional, and national levels, along with results reported from outside entities such as independent third parties or regulators. The scope statement provides context for the overall opinion by specifying the time period, activities, limitations, and other variables that describe the boundaries of the overall opinion.

When reviewing engagement conclusions and other communications on which the overall opinion is based, the CAE ensures that such conclusions and other communicated results were based on sufficient, reliable, relevant, and useful information. The CAE then summarizes the information on which the overall opinion is based. In addition, the CAE identifies relevant risk or control frameworks or other criteria used as a basis for the overall opinion.

Upon consideration of the relevant information, the CAE issues an overall opinion, using clear and concise language, and articulates how the opinion relates to the strategies, objectives, and risks of the organization. The communication should include the six elements listed in the Interpretation of Standard 2450.

If the overall opinion is unfavorable, the CAE must explain the reasons supporting this conclusion.

Finally, the CAE decides how to communicate the overall opinion (verbally or in writing). Overall opinions are typically communicated in writing, although there is no requirement in the Standards to do so. Implementation Guide 2440—Disseminating Results provides further guidance on additional considerations for communications.

It is important to note that the CAE is not required to issue an overall opinion; issuance of such an opinion is at the discretion of the organization and would be discussed with senior management and the board. However, when an overall opinion is requested, Standard 2450 provides additional information to support the CAE in the requirements related to communicating an overall opinion.

Considerations for Demonstrating Conformance

For written overall opinions, a copy of the opinion is typically sufficient to demonstrate conformance. For overall opinions that are delivered verbally, conformance may be demonstrated through the CAE's outline, speaking notes, slides, or similar documents. Additional materials that may demonstrate conformance with Standard 2450 include final engagement communications and external communications on which the overall opinion is based, memos, emails, board or other meeting agendas, and meeting minutes.

> ## Standard 2500 – Monitoring Progress

The chief audit executive must establish and maintain a system to monitor the disposition of results communicated to management.

▶ IG2500 – Monitoring Progress

Getting Started

To fulfill this standard, the chief audit executive (CAE) starts by attaining a clear understanding of the type of information and level of detail the board and senior management expect with regard to the internal audit activity's monitoring of the results of engagements. Results typically refer to the observations developed in assurance and consulting engagements that have been communicated to management for corrective action.

Given that periodic interactions will be required with the management responsible for implementing corrective actions, it is generally helpful to solicit management's input on ways to create an effective and efficient monitoring process.

Further, the CAE may want to benchmark with other CAEs or compliance functions that monitor outstanding issues to identify leading practices that have proven effectiveness. These discussions may address areas such as:

- The levels of automation and detail.
- The types of observations monitored (i.e., all or just higher risk observations).
- How and with what frequency the status of outstanding corrective actions is determined.
- When internal audit independently confirms the effectiveness of corrective actions.
- The frequency, style, and level of reporting performed.

Considerations for Implementation

Monitoring processes can be sophisticated or rather simple, depending on a number of factors, including the size and complexity of the audit organization and the availability of exception tracking software. Whether sophisticated or simple, it is important for the CAE to develop a process that captures the relevant observations, agreed corrective action, and current status. For outstanding observations, the information tracked and captured typically includes:

- The observations communicated to management and their relative risk rating.
- The nature of the agreed corrective actions.
- The timing/deadlines/age of the corrective actions and changes in target dates.
- The management/process owner responsible for each corrective action.
- The current status of corrective actions, and whether internal audit has confirmed the status.

Often, the CAE will develop or purchase a tool, mechanism, or system to track, monitor, and report on such information. Based on information provided to internal audit by the responsible management, the status of the corrective actions is updated in the system periodically and often directly by management using a shared exception tracking system.

The frequency and approach to monitoring (the extent of audit staff work to verify that corrective action was taken) is determined based on the CAE's professional judgment, as well as the expectations set by the board and senior management. For example, some CAEs may choose to inquire periodically, such as quarterly, about the status of all corrective actions that were due to be completed in the prior period. Others may choose to perform periodic follow-up engagements for audits with significant recommendations to specifically assess the quality of the corrective actions taken. Others may choose to follow up on outstanding actions during a future audit scheduled in the same area of the organization. The approach is determined based on the adjudged level of risk, as well as the availability of resources.

Similarly, the form of reporting is determined based on the CAE's judgment and the agreed expectations. Some CAEs will report the status of every observation for every engagement in a detailed manner. Others will report only on observations rated higher risk, perhaps summarized by business process or executive owner, noting statistics such as percentage of corrective actions on track, overdue, and completed on time. In some instances, the CAE may be asked to report on not just whether the corrective action has been completed, but also whether the action taken has corrected the underlying issue. Capturing and measuring positive improvement based on the execution of corrective actions is considered a leading practice.

Considerations for Demonstrating Conformance

Conformance is typically evidenced by the existence of a routinely updated exception tracking system, which could be a spreadsheet, database, or other tool that contains the prior audit observations, associated corrective action plan, status, and internal audit's confirmation, as described above. Also, there are typically corrective action status reports prepared for senior management and the board.

IG2600 – Communicating the Acceptance of Risks

Getting Started

To be successful in implementing this standard, the chief audit executive (CAE) must first understand the organization's view of and tolerance for various types of organizational risks. Organizations vary by how much and what types of risk they consider acceptable. For example, some organizations may accept higher levels of financial risk—taking actions such as expanding into a new geography with an unstable government; or making a material investment in an exciting new product that has a relatively small probability of success, but high reward if successful. Other organizations are more averse to such financial risks, avoiding such situations. Further, organizations consider different factors in determining the level of acceptable risk; for example, the potential impact and likelihood of the risk event, the vulnerability of the organization, and the length of time it takes management to resolve an unacceptable risk.

If the organization has a formal risk management policy, which may include a risk acceptance process, it is important that the CAE and the internal audit activity understand it.

As required by Standard 2500, the CAE also must establish and maintain a system for monitoring the disposition of the results of internal audits.

It is also helpful for the CAE to know how higher risk issues are typically communicated within the organization. Existing policies may define a preferred communication approach; for example, an organization's risk management policy may discuss timeliness, hierarchy of reporting, and similar considerations.

Considerations for Implementation

In monitoring the disposition of results and associated corrective actions, the CAE may become aware of high risk observations that are not timely corrected or may represent more risk than the organization would normally tolerate and are therefore unacceptable to the organization.

▶ Standard 2600 – Communicating the Acceptance of Risks

When the chief audit executive concludes that management has accepted a level of risk that may be unacceptable to the organization, the chief audit executive must discuss the matter with senior management. If the chief audit executive determines that the matter has not been resolved, the chief audit executive must communicate the matter to the board.

Interpretation:

The identification of risk accepted by management may be observed through an assurance or consulting engagement, monitoring progress on actions taken by management as a result of prior engagements, or other means. It is not the responsibility of the chief audit executive to resolve the risk.

However, the ongoing monitoring process is not the only way a CAE identifies unacceptable risk. An effective CAE employs several ways to stay abreast of organizational risks. For example, the CAE may receive information from members of the internal audit activity regarding significant risks they have identified during their assurance or consulting engagements. Or the organization may employ an enterprise risk management (ERM) process to identify and monitor significant risks, and the CAE may be involved with that process. Further, by building and maintaining a collaborative, communicative network with management, the CAE may become aware of an emerging risk area in the organization. CAEs also strive to keep up with industry trends and regulatory changes to help them recognize potential and emerging risks.

Regardless of how the unacceptable risk is identified, if the CAE recognizes the risk as being at such a high level that the organization would normally not tolerate it, and if the CAE believes that the risk is not being mitigated to an acceptable level, then he or she is required to communicate this situation to senior management. Prior to such a communication, the CAE typically discusses the issue with the members of management responsible for the risk area, to share concerns, understand management's perspective, and reach an agreed path to resolve the risk. However, if such an agreement isn't reached, then the CAE must escalate the concern to senior management. And, after a similar discussion with senior management, if the risk remains unresolved, then the CAE must communicate the issue to the board. It is then the board's decision how to address the concern with management.

The CAE uses judgment to determine how best and how quickly to communicate such matters to whom, based on the issue's nature, urgency, potential ramifications, and any policies that may be in place. For example, should the general counsel be consulted, such as when a law or regulation may have been violated? And should the risk be communicated in private to a senior executive or in a cross-functional meeting with many subject matter specialists in attendance?

This standard applies to highly significant risks that the CAE judges to be beyond the organization's tolerance level. These may include:

- Those that may harm the organization's reputation.
- Those that could harm people.
- Those that would result in significant regulatory fines, limitations on business conduct, or other financial or contractual penalties.
- Material misstatements.
- Fraud or other illegal acts.
- Significant impediments to achieving strategic objectives.

Considerations for Demonstrating Conformance

Evidence of conformance could be found in minutes of meetings where a significant risk issue was discussed with the executive management team, the board, or a risk committee. If the CAE communicates the unacceptable risk situation through one-on-one meetings or during a private session, a memo to file can be used to document the steps taken to alert management and the board. Also, an indirect indication of conformance is a policy in the internal audit manual that describes the requirements of this standard and the organization's reporting process.

Glossary

Add Value

The internal audit activity adds value to the organization (and its stakeholders) when it provides objective and relevant assurance, and contributes to the effectiveness and efficiency of governance, risk management, and control processes.

Adequate Control

Present if management has planned and organized (designed) in a manner that provides reasonable assurance that the organization's risks have been managed effectively and that the organization's goals and objectives will be achieved efficiently and economically.

Assurance Services

An objective examination of evidence for the purpose of providing an independent assessment on governance, risk management, and control processes for the organization. Examples may include financial, performance, compliance, system security, and due diligence engagements.

Board

The highest level governing body (e.g., a board of directors, a supervisory board, or a board of governors or trustees) charged with the responsibility to direct and/or oversee the organization's activities and hold senior management accountable. Although governance arrangements vary among jurisdictions and sectors, typically the board includes members who are not part of management. If a board does not exist, the word "board" in the *Standards* refers to a group or person charged with governance of the organization. Furthermore, "board" in the *Standards* may refer to a committee or another body to which the governing body has delegated certain functions (e.g., an audit committee).

Charter

The internal audit charter is a formal document that defines the internal audit activity's purpose, authority, and responsibility. The internal audit charter establishes the internal audit activity's position within the organization; authorizes access to records, personnel, and physical properties relevant to the performance of engagements; and defines the scope of internal audit activities.

Chief Audit Executive

Chief audit executive describes the role of a person in a senior position responsible for effectively managing the internal audit activity in accordance with the internal audit charter and the mandatory elements of the International Professional Practices Framework. The chief audit executive or others reporting to the chief audit executive will have appropriate professional certifications and qualifications. The specific job title and/or responsibilities of the chief audit executive may vary across organizations.

Code of Ethics

The Code of Ethics of The Institute of Internal Auditors are Principles relevant to the profession and practice of internal auditing, and Rules of Conduct that describe behavior expected of internal auditors. The Code of Ethics applies to both parties and entities that provide internal audit services. The purpose of the Code of Ethics is to promote an ethical culture in the global profession of internal auditing.

Compliance

Adherence to policies, plans, procedures, laws, regulations, contracts, or other requirements.

Conflict of Interest

Any relationship that is, or appears to be, not in the best interest of the organization. A conflict of interest would prejudice an individual's ability to perform his or her duties and responsibilities objectively.

Consulting Services

Advisory and related client service activities, the nature and scope of which are agreed with the client, are intended to add value and improve an organization's governance, risk management, and control processes without the internal auditor assuming management responsibility. Examples include counsel, advice, facilitation, and training.

Control

Any action taken by management, the board, and other parties to manage risk and increase the likelihood that established objectives and goals will be achieved. Management plans, organizes, and directs the performance of sufficient actions to provide reasonable assurance that objectives and goals will be achieved.

Control Environment

The attitude and actions of the board and management regarding the importance of control within the organization. The control environment provides the discipline and structure for the achievement of the primary objectives of the system of internal control. The control environment includes the following elements:

- Integrity and ethical values.
- Management's philosophy and operating style.
- Organizational structure.
- Assignment of authority and responsibility.
- Human resource policies and practices.
- Competence of personnel.

Control Processes

The policies, procedures (both manual and automated), and activities that are part of a control framework, designed and operated to ensure that risks are contained within the level that an organization is willing to accept.

Core Principles for the Professional Practice of Internal Auditing

The Core Principles for the Professional Practice of Internal Auditing are the foundation for the International Professional Practices Framework and support internal audit effectiveness.

Engagement

A specific internal audit assignment, task, or review activity, such as an internal audit, control self-assessment review, fraud examination, or consultancy. An engagement may include multiple tasks or activities designed to accomplish a specific set of related objectives.

Engagement Objectives

Broad statements developed by internal auditors that define intended engagement accomplishments.

Engagement Opinion

The rating, conclusion, and/or other description of results of an individual internal audit engagement, relating to those aspects within the objectives and scope of the engagement.

Engagement Work Program

A document that lists the procedures to be followed during an engagement, designed to achieve the engagement plan.

External Service Provider

A person or firm outside of the organization that has special knowledge, skill, and experience in a particular discipline.

Fraud

Any illegal act characterized by deceit, concealment, or violation of trust. These acts are not dependent upon the threat of violence or physical force. Frauds are perpetrated by parties and organizations to obtain money, property, or services; to avoid payment or loss of services; or to secure personal or business advantage.

Governance

The combination of processes and structures implemented by the board to inform, direct, manage, and monitor the activities of the organization toward the achievement of its objectives.

Impairment

Impairment to organizational independence and individual objectivity may include personal conflict of interest, scope limitations, restrictions on access to records, personnel, and properties, and resource limitations (funding).

Independence

The freedom from conditions that threaten the ability of the internal audit activity to carry out internal audit responsibilities in an unbiased manner.

Information Technology Controls

Controls that support business management and governance as well as provide general and technical controls over information technology infrastructures such as applications, information, infrastructure, and people.

Information Technology Governance

Consists of the leadership, organizational structures, and processes that ensure that the enterprise's information technology supports the organization's strategies and objectives.

Internal Audit Activity

A department, division, team of consultants, or other practitioner(s) that provides independent, objective assurance and consulting services designed to add value and improve an organization's operations. The internal audit activity helps an organization accomplish its objectives by bringing a systematic, disciplined approach to evaluate and improve the effectiveness of governance, risk management and control processes.

International Professional Practices Framework

The conceptual framework that organizes the authoritative guidance promulgated by The IIA. Authoritative guidance is composed of two categories—(1) mandatory and (2) recommended.

Must

The *Standards* use the word "must" to specify an unconditional requirement.

Objectivity

An unbiased mental attitude that allows internal auditors to perform engagements in such a manner that they believe in their work product and that no quality compromises are made. Objectivity requires that internal auditors do not subordinate their judgment on audit matters to others.

Overall Opinion

The rating, conclusion, and/or other description of results provided by the chief audit executive addressing, at a broad level, governance, risk management, and/or control processes of the organization. An overall opinion is the professional judgment of the chief audit executive based on the results of a number of individual engagements and other activities for a specific time interval.

Risk

The possibility of an event occurring that will have an impact on the achievement of objectives. Risk is measured in terms of impact and likelihood.

Risk Appetite

The level of risk that an organization is willing to accept.

Risk Management

A process to identify, assess, manage, and control potential events or situations to provide reasonable assurance regarding the achievement of the organization's objectives.

Should

The *Standards* use the word "should" where conformance is expected unless, when applying professional judgment, circumstances justify deviation.

Significance

The relative importance of a matter within the context in which it is being considered, including quantitative and qualitative factors, such as magnitude, nature, effect, relevance, and impact. Professional judgment assists internal auditors when evaluating the significance of matters within the context of the relevant objectives.

Standard

A professional pronouncement promulgated by the International Internal Audit Standards Board that delineates the requirements for performing a broad range of internal audit activities, and for evaluating internal audit performance.

Technology-based Audit Techniques

Any automated audit tool, such as generalized audit software, test data generators, computerized audit programs, specialized audit utilities, and computer-assisted audit techniques (CAATs).